# Tourist Travel Guide to Spain 2023

Discover Spain's Deep Culture, Scenic Beauty, and Hidden Gems in 2023

© **Taylor M. Ross**

All rights reserved. No part of this publication may be reproduced, distributed, or transmitted in any form or by any means, including photocopying, recording, or other electronic or mechanical methods, without the prior written permission of the publisher, except in the case of brief quotations embodied in critical reviews and certain other noncommercial uses permitted by copyright law.

Copyright © Taylor M. Ross, 2023

# Table of Content

History of Spain

Government of Spain

SPAIN'S GEOGRAPHY AND CLIMATE

Cultural Highlights of Spain

Tapas

Los Sieta

Flamenco

Semana Santa

The Valencian Fallas

Festa Major de Gràcia

Tamborrada de San Sebastián

The Magos Reyes

Cordoba's Festival de Los Patios

Jerez May Horse Fair

Carnival

Christmas and the New Year

Conclusion

**Chapter One**

Fun Facts About Spain!

The first global empire was Spain

There is a Royal Family in Spain

5-Day Itinerary For You!

Traveling in Spain

**Chapter two**

Planning Your Trip to Spain: A Comprehensive Guide

Exploring Spanish Cities:

Top Madrid Attractions

Art & Cultural Scene in Madrid

Gastronomy and Nightlife in Madrid

Barcelona: The Mediterranean Gem

**Chapter Three**

Exploring the Gothic Quarter:

Immerse Yourself in Barcelona's Historic Heart

**Chapter four:**

Spain's Natural Beauty

Marbella: A Glamourous Costa del Sol City

Exploring the Charming White Villages

The Canary Islands: A Piece of Atlantic Paradise

**Chapter five**

Immersive Cultural Experiences: Unveiling the Soul of Spain

Understanding the Art of Bullfighting

Wine and Cuisine

Spain's Wine and Gastronomy: A Flavorful Journey

Wine Regions and Tastings in Spain

**Chapter six:**

Spain Accommodation Options: Choosing the Right Place to Stay

**Chapter Seven**

Using Language and Expressions

## INTRODUCTION

We cordially invite you to explore the "Tourist Travel Guide to Spain 2023: Discover the Rich Culture, Scenic Beauty, and Hidden Gems of Spain in 2023." Your passport to a memorable trip across one of Europe's most alluring nations is this thorough handbook. Spain provides a treasure trove of activities to satiate any traveler's wanderlust, whether you're an active backpacker, a history buff, a foodie, or just looking for a sun-drenched break.

Spain still charms tourists in 2023 with its vivacious culture, breathtaking scenery, and rich tapestry of history. This guide will take you on a virtual tour of Spain's famous sites, engrossing you in the tales and traditions that have created the country, from the spectacular architecture of Gaud in Barcelona to the majestic Alhambra in Granada.

You'll learn about Spain's diverse geography as you start your Spanish trip. Spain's landscapes are as diverse as they are beautiful, ranging from the Mediterranean coast's sun-drenched beaches to the Pyrenees Mountains' rough beauty. Discover the alluring Andalusian countryside, stroll through charming towns hidden in La Rioja's undulating hills, or be amazed by the magnificent cliffs that line Galicia's Atlantic coast.

Spain is a colorful patchwork of many cultures and regional customs, not simply a beautiful landscape. Discover the essence of Spanish culture by seeing flamenco performances in Seville's winding lanes, taking part in Las Fallas celebrations in Valencia, or viewing the spine-tingling Semana Santa processions in Malaga. This guide will make sure you don't miss any of the interesting festivities and customs that make up Spain's rich cultural history.

Without sampling some of Spain's famed food, a trip to the country would not be complete. Spanish cuisine is a delight for the senses, from the tempting aromas of tapas to the delicious paella. Explore the vineyards of La Rioja, which produces some of the world's greatest wines, sample fresh seafood in the seaside villages of Galicia, or indulge in the smokey flavors of Basque cuisine in San Sebastian. Prepare yourself for a gourmet journey as we lead you through the top eating establishments and provide insights into local delicacies and age-old recipes.

We have painstakingly assembled a thorough guide, "Tourist Travel Guide to Spain 2023," to assist you in navigating Spain's captivating cities, finding undiscovered treasures, and making lifelong experiences. This manual will make sure that every element of your trip is smooth and pleasurable, with helpful advice on lodging and transportation as well as thorough itineraries for various kinds of tourists.

Therefore, this book is your dependable travel companion whether your dreams include wandering through the medieval alleyways of Toledo, soaking in the sun on the beaches of Ibiza, or discovering the architectural marvels of Barcelona. Prepare to be enthralled by the beauty of Spain's towns, landscapes, and cultural treasures as well as the warmth and kindness of the Spanish people. Also, prepare to indulge in delectable food. Let the "Tourist Travel Guide to Spain 2023" serve as your starting point for an enjoyable journey around this amazing nation.

**History of Spain**

The current period Some of the earliest archeological sites in Europe are found in Spain, which has been home to human habitation for thousands of years along with the Iberian Peninsula. The Phoenicians, Greeks, Carthaginians, and Celts all arrived in the area around the ninth century BCE, but the Romans took up residence by the second century BCE. Roman habitation in Spain continued until the seventh century, although the Visigoths, who came in the fifth century, occupied many of the Roman sites. The Moors from North Africa invaded Spain in 711 and drove the Visigoths to the north. Despite many efforts to drive them away, the Moors stayed in the region until 1492. The U.S. Department of State claims that by

1512, Spain as we know it today had been united.

Because of the riches it had amassed via its discovery of North and South America by the 16th century, Spain was the most powerful nation in all of Europe. However, it had been involved in several battles by the century's end, and its strength had decreased. It was occupied by France in the early 1800s, and during the 19th century, it took part in several conflicts, notably the Spanish-American War (1898). At this time, several Spanish colonies abroad also rose in rebellion and won their freedom. Due to these issues, the nation experienced dictatorship from 1923 to 1931. When the Second Republic was established in 1931, this period came to an end. As tensions and unrest persisted in Spain, the Spanish Civil War broke out in July 1936.

General Francisco Franco seized power in Spain when the civil war was completed in 1939. Spain embraced Axis power policies while being ostensibly neutral at the start of World War II; as a result, it was ostracized by the Allies after the war. The Mutual Defense Assistance Agreement between Spain and the United States was signed in 1953, and in 1955, Spain became a member of the UN.

As a result of these worldwide collaborations, Spain's economy was finally able to start expanding after being isolated from most of Europe and the rest of the globe up until that point. Spain had a sophisticated economy by the 1960s and 1970s, and in the late 1970s, it started the transition to a more democratic system of governance.

**Government of Spain**

Currently, King Juan Carlos I serves as both the head of state and the head of government of Spain, which is ruled as a parliamentary monarchy. A bicameral legislative body, the General Courts (consisting of the Senate) and the Congress of Deputies, are also present in Spain. The Supreme Court, sometimes known as the Tribunal Supremo, is a part of the Spanish legal system. For local government, the nation is split up into 17 autonomous communities.

## SPAIN'S GEOGRAPHY AND CLIMATE

The primary influence on the climate of Spain is its location on the Iberian Peninsula. Large air masses that travel across the peninsula from north to south influence the weather according to the seasons. Spain is the most mountainous nation in Europe; there are 5 mountain ranges on its soil, and a sizeable portion is covered by plateaus that are 600–900 meters above sea level. The climate is divided into distinct zones due to the terrain and the semi-island's geographic position.

Spain has 4 distinct climate zones. Oceanic - along the Bay of Biscay's coast, from the Pyrenees to Galicia. It is characterized by regular rains and comfortable temperatures. Mountain, on the ridges of the semi-island, with moderate summers and subzero winters. The majority of central Spain's plateaus are continental, with summer temperatures averaging up to +45 degrees and winter temperatures averaging up to –10 degrees. The whole Mediterranean Sea coast, from Cadiz to the French border, has a Mediterranean climate.

The dry Mediterranean climatic zone, which has a variety of unique features, includes the province of Alicante. Less than 300 mm of rainfall occurs annually. This explains why people claim that it is always sunny here. The air is dryer and somewhat warmer throughout the summer. The temperature fluctuates very little below +10 degrees Celsius on an annual average basis, hovering between 15 and 18 degrees. The temperature never rises over +34 degrees throughout the summer. The beach season here lasts all year long, therefore you can be sure that this is Benidorm if you see vacationers sunning on the beach in January on the European news. By September, the water often reaches a temperature of 28 degrees, and in the winter, it seldom falls below 13. Over the Christmas break, a lot of people go to the Costa Blanca to enjoy the sunshine.

If you prefer to ski in the winter, the Sierra Nevada mountain range is 350 miles from Alicante, the Pyrenees are 500 km distant, and resorts in Andorra are 650 km away. All of these distances are easily traveled on decent highways. The opulent amenities found at mountain resorts include a wide range of hotels, ski lifts, equipment rental services, and instructor services. Everything is set up for a good vacation.

As a result, Spain's location, temperature, and very nature all contribute to the Spanish kingdom's high level of life.

If your vacation is scheduled for the winter, don't be unhappy and prepare yourself for the fact that you will have to take a nap in bitter cold or, at best, someplace in the country's south, where the weather won't be ideal for a complete nap by the sea. All of this is the result of our ignorance and stereotyped tendencies; those who regularly take vacations in various regions of the world are aware that the location you choose affects how well you can relax.

**Cultural Highlights of Spain**

Spain is renowned as a nation for its amazing history, varied regional cultures, and distinctive way of life. Flamenco and the running of the bulls are just two of the country's unique charms that draw tourists from all over the globe.

Spain has the oldest civilization in the world, according to anthropologists. It has a strong Iberian and Roman Celtic influence. Also having an impact on Spain are the Greek, Carthaginian, Roman, and Phoenician civilizations. They had a religious and linguistic effect on Spanish culture. Hispania is a magnificent example of Roman heritage. They saw Hispania as a center for administration, law, and politics. The whole continent has been impacted by Spain's cultural activity. This country gave rise to the Spanish language. Furthermore, notable poets and authors like Pablo Picasso have contributed to the fame of Spanish culture.

Spain has a lot of intriguing and distinctive customs. Some of these customs have a significant impact on Latin American nations as well. These fantastic cultural activities may be found in Spain. Take a glance, and you'll see that they are great!

**Tapas**

In Spain, tapas are a popular tiny snack served as an appetizer. Typically on weekends, people eat appetizers before lunch and supper at bars. According to Tapas's history, during the reign of King Alfonso X of Castile,

He became sick. He consumed wine and tapas as a kind of therapy. He healed by consuming tapas and wine, therefore he advised tapas and wine at all the inns.

Spanish folks eat dinner later, usually around 9 or 10. They have plenty of time to eat snacks before meals as a result. People consume this food at bars, therefore each one cooks it differently. They utilize tortillas, tomato, chorizo, ham, cheese, and fried potatoes with a hot sauce.

The most fascinating aspect of this custom is when patrons of some establishments toss toothpicks and napkins on the ground. The more delicious the tapas, the more napkins, and toothpicks will be dropped on the ground.

**Los Sieta**

La Siesta translates to "the nap." It is a well-known custom in Spain. Although everyone is aware of this custom, few individuals follow it. Spanish folks eat a large lunch since they don't eat much at breakfast or evening. Therefore, blood flows to the stomach of the individuals after a big meal to aid with dyspepsia.

One becomes sleepy and exhausted as a result. The fact that Spanish people suffer high temperatures around noon is the other reason for having a nap. They are thus unable to engage in any kind of mental or physical activity. As a result, La Siesta became a custom. The shops and businesses are shut down for naps.

During the warmest portion of the day, firm employees take a lunch break and snooze at home. Due to their desire to buy at that hour of the day, the foreigners dislike this ritual.

**Flamenco**

Flamenco consists of guitar instrumentals, dance, and singing. It is linked to the Andalusian Roma or southern Spanish gypsies. Flamenco's origins may be traced to the Roma migration from Rajasthan between the ninth and fourteenth centuries. These immigrants left behind a rich musical heritage that included a variety of songs and dances as well as the usage of bells, tambourines, and wooden castanets.

When they arrived in Spain, they came into contact with the Moors and Sephardic Jews, which led to the creation of a new art form known as flamenco. The finest thing about Flamenco music is that, despite the influence of other cultures, its melodies and lyrics are entirely Spanish. Flamenco dancers like practicing their dance and put a lot of effort into it. People like how the dance can express itself differently depending on the song's mood.

**Semana Santa**

In Spain, Semana Santa is observed as a holy week. People create a procession and leave their houses to participate in the festivities. During the week leading up to Easter, these processions go across the city. The fundamental idea of the cultural activity is the same, even if the style and atmosphere of these processions vary from city to city.

In daily processions, a representative of a religious group is present. When they arrive at the town's main cathedral, they carry flags before turning around and returning. This ritual has been observed by Spaniards for many years, and they continue to commemorate it with the same fervor as they did in the past.

People in numerous Spanish towns participate in this cultural activity's celebrations, although Seville and Malaga's celebrations are the most well-known. The Semana Santa procession is also supported by the towns of Valladolid and Leon.

Paella

A well-known rice dish from Spain is paella. It is often regarded as the national dish of Spain. People prepare dishes using meat or fish. This meal was created by Valencia City, and the name paella is taken from the Latin word patella and an ancient French word. This meal is prepared by Spaniards on huge occasions.

The classic Paella meal comprises meat and vegetables, however, in Spain's coastal regions, beef is used in place of fish. Despite being a hybrid form and a variation on the standard Parella, the seafood and meat combo.

The fact that this recipe just requires one pan is what I find most astounding. various pans are used to make various dishes in several European nations. Furthermore, if you are preparing a single meal, you must also prepare other dishes that are served separately. You don't need to prepare side dishes for paella, however.

**The Valencian Fallas**

For five days and nights in March, Valencians and visitors from all over the world congregated in the city's streets for a street celebration known as the fire festival. In honor of Saint Joseph, the revered patron saint of carpenters, this customary event is held. Initially, carpenters would light candles while working on wooden boards.

This custom is observed in the spring to symbolize the passing of the shorter winter days. Additionally, they dress the planks to give them identities similar to ninots that resemble famous people and leaders.
Brass bands and firecrackers erupted during this custom, illuminating the city. It's interesting how this ritual involves a lot of activity, processions, and pyrotechnics. The most astounding aspect of this custom is that pyrotechnics are used to make ninots in the plaza Ayuntamiento when firemen are on duty and the streetlights are turned out. This well-known custom is a part of humanity's intangible cultural heritage, according to UNESCO.

**Festa Major de Gràcia**

The Festa Major de Gracia is a rather new event. It came from Villa de Gracia, a little community that no longer exists. This community was renowned for its laborers, small shopkeepers, and artists. To honor San Isidro, who passed away on August 15, people hold this event on May 15th. The winner of this cultural competition between the streets is decided by the judges. The street's residents decide on a theme, such as a fairytale or a movie. As a result, they embellish the roadway in keeping with the motif.

They don't reveal the street's concept. People adorn the streets with love and creativity the day before August 15th. The competition is conducted on the corresponding day, and the jury selects the winner after one week. Garcia's neighbors, however, take full advantage of the festive streets at this time.

**La Tomatinos**

Thousands of people converge on the little village of Bunol every year at the end of August. With 9,000 residents, it is a tiny town in Valencia. A tomato battle known as La Tomatina draws over 40,000 visitors to this hamlet. People participating in the celebration are throwing overripe tomatoes, turning the streets of Bunol into rivers of tomato paste during the battle.

As a result, it is the biggest tomato battle ever. This battle goes on for an hour. About 150,000 overripe tomatoes are used in this battle. A small group of people began this cultural practice in 1940 by throwing a vegetable during a street procession. A brawl resulted in some person lighting a fire. People, however, found enjoyment in this action, and they began bringing their tomatoes and starting tomato battles every year.

### (Pamplona Bull Run) San Fermin

In Irunea/Pamplona, San Fermin's cultural celebrations are held. It is situated in the Navarra area. Every year, people celebrate it from July 6 to July 14. The running of the bulls has made them quite well-known. Bulls race through the streets and join the runners in the bull ring.

In honor of San Fermin, a Navarran saint, people celebrate this event. People are not aware of the religious component, however. People from all around the globe are now enjoying this hobby. The most crucial aspect of this event is the pleasure and fun.

The Enceirro is the festival's main attraction. Bulls from outside the city come during this event to intimidate people. At eight in the morning, when the bell at the church of San Cernin rings, this celebration begins at the cage in Calle Santo Domingo.

The cage is located 825 meters from the bullring. The bulls must thus run. The running lasts for three to four minutes, but if a bull is not with its buddy, it may occasionally last for 10 minutes.

**Tamborrada de San Sebastián**

A cultural event is the Tamborrada de San Sebastian. On January 20th, people commemorate this holiday. Young and elderly come out of their houses to participate in this highly intriguing cultural celebration. This cultural event is connected to the story of the city when San Sebastian withstood raids from the French and English.

In this practice, city dwellers use spoons, sticks, and frying pans to make noise in an attempt to imitate the troops. This custom has San Sabastian origins and has gained popularity over time.

People just utilize drums at the beginning of this cultural activity, and they dress whichever they choose. With time, they begin to dress traditionally, even in military garb from Napoleon's time, and prepare their preferred foods. They then begin to march in the direction of the famed Plaza de la Constitution. At that location, the San Sebastian flag is raised at midnight.

## The Magos Reyes

Old St. Nick refers to the three monarchs as a religious legend in Spain. English speakers refer to this cultural practice as "the three wise men." According to the teachings of the Bible, these three men journeyed to Bethlehem from all over the globe to present the gift to the infant Jesus. There is still controversy as to whether or not these individuals were kings, but their custom of bestowing presents endures.

On January 5, people commemorate this day. People place their empty shoes near a window on this day's evening in the hopes that gifts and delicacies would fill them. Additionally, some children offer the monarchs three glasses of warm milk, while others leave hay and grass for the hungry camels. The youngsters were delighted to discover their shoes the other day filled with several toys and sweets.

## Cordoba's Festival de Los Patios

The Cordoba Patios Festival is an enjoyable Spanish cultural event. This is a holiday observed during the first week of Spain. Additionally, it is a long-standing custom in Cordoba City. Patios are just country yards, and this cultural practice entails adorning the courtyards with lovely flowers and plants.

In 1918, the first cultural event on the Patio took place. Behind the city's doors and walls, there are hidden courtyards that people utilize. People invite guests to visit their lovely rural yards as part of this custom.

To participate in this celebration, many people traveled to Cordoba from all over the globe. This custom is not only about flora. You may go to Cordoba, however, for its incredible history, delectable cuisine, and stunning scenery.

## Jerez May Horse Fair

Feria del Caballo is the name of the horse fair held in Jerez. This customary event is observed during the first or second week of May. It is an exciting and happy event. As a result, everyone is eager to attend the Gonzalez Hontoria fairground. This horse-friendly ground has a surface size of 52,000 square meters.

The fairground has a more contemporary name. It debuted in 1903. It was determined at the time that societies and people should present their arguments. 200 casitas were therefore constructed in the city. The farolillos, or bright la Cordoba patios, are exquisitely ornamented. Most of the cases are private, such as Cordoba Patios. Only those who are invited may visit them. The entire public is welcome to visit and enjoy Jeraz.

## Carnival

Spain not only celebrates the aforementioned holidays but has a thriving cultural life. You may take advantage of adjacent carnivals in any city in Spain. Although each city in Spain celebrates the festivities uniquely, you can still take in the stunning costumes, mouthwatering cuisine, and vibrant music and dancing in the country's atmosphere. varied cultures have varied ways of celebrating Carnival, but Tenerife's is the most spectacular. The carnivals in Cadiz and Sitges come after Tenerife.

## Christmas and the New Year

The best season of the year is Christmas. The same is true for Spain in this remark. how Christmas is observed by Spaniards. Everybody in the nation enjoys their holidays, and they light up the city with sparkling decorations. Spain's temperate climate makes it more enjoyable for the locals since it doesn't become as chilly as other places.

On Christmas Eve, people bring their family members and friends around for drinks and hours of conversation. Additionally, on Christmas Day, individuals prepare delectable meals and invite friends and family. Children anticipate Santa Claus's arrival and his gift-giving visit.

**Conclusion**

The various cultures of the globe are appreciated by Spaniards. The USA is home to one of the biggest Spanish-speaking populations. It's crucial to connect with Spanish-speaking groups in Spanish if you want to do so successfully. You may cope with Spanish cultural events appropriately by using the Spanish language to comprehend them.

## Chapter One

**Fun Facts About Spain!**

**Spain Is The Only European Country To Have A Physical Border With An African Country**

We start with one of the most entertaining geographical facts about Spain, which is that it has a land border, not a maritime one, with an African nation. This nation is Morocco. How is this possible? because Spain still retains a little enclave named Ceuta on the continent of Africa. Since the first century BC, this city has been strategically significant and changed ownership many times until coming under Spanish control in 1668.

**The first global empire was Spain**

Talk about one of the fascinating facts about Spain is that it was once the most powerful nation on earth. The Spanish advanced the

Portuguese commercial empire by many notches while establishing themselves in North, Central, and South America and dominating the Philippines for more than 300 years. They amassed wealth for themselves and left a sizable cultural heritage and a sizable number of Spanish-speaking people in their wake.

There Are Many Islands in Spain.

Any plan for Spain will include visits to certain beaches. Spain has territories outside of the Iberian Peninsula as well. There are the well-known Balearic Islands in the Mediterranean Sea, which naturally include the very well-known party island of Ibiza, and then there are the Canary Islands, which are located far out in the Atlantic Ocean.
Just off Morocco's Mediterranean coast are the Plazas de Soberana as well.

**There is a Royal Family in Spain**

If you believed there wasn't, you should be aware of this interesting truth about Spain. King Felipe VI is the reigning king as of 2014 in this constitutional monarchy. Following the removal of the reigning monarch, Isabella II, in the Glorious Revolution of 1868, democracy was established.

**The oldest restaurant in the world is in Madrid**

Any information about Spanish cuisine makes us want to visit the country once again and sample all of its delectable offerings. This one is about El Restaurante Botn, which Guinness World Records has officially acknowledged as the oldest restaurant in the world. When visiting the Spanish capital, you must see this location, which first opened its doors in 1725.
For five centuries, Muslims ruled over Spain.
Invading groups from North Africa known as "Moors" entered Spain around 711 AD. It was known as Al-Andalus. The language, culture, and art of Spain were subsequently influenced

by Arabic and Islamic civilization over a significant period until the invaders were eventually driven out in 1492. This is felt most keenly in Andalusia's southern portion.

**Spain Has a Few Quite Notable Festivals**

You're aware of the Running of the Bulls, aren't you? Every year, Pamplona hosts this. You probably aren't aware that it is a component of a larger, nine-day Saint Fermin celebration. Even if there are other "bull-runs," that one is the most well-known.

La Tomatina, the largest food battle in the world, is held somewhere else. When a man began tossing tomatoes at his companions in 1945, it all got started. The celebration was outlawed in the 1950s but was brought back in 1957 when locals performed a funeral for it, replete with a coffin-bound tomato.

Spain hosted one-half of the first Earth Sandwich in 2006.

What the hell? As a result, a few individuals in Spain and a few individuals in New Zealand put baguettes on the ground when a radio DJ questioned if it was conceivable. The outcome was an Earth Sandwich with miles and miles of molten lava and a burning core as the filler.

**In the New Year, we eat grapes.**

While for many, the countdown to the New Year involves becoming very inebriated before, after, or during it, in Spain, we have one delicate custom that we enjoy: eating grapes. To be exact, twelve. It's supposed that if you can eat a grape at each precise stroke of midnight, you'll be lucky for the rest of the year.

In Spain, a tooth mouse by the name of Ratoncito Perez serves as the replacement for the tooth fairy.

**There is no tooth fairy in Spain, which is a strange truth.**

That's hardly the strangest thing, I suppose. They have a tooth... mouse instead of a tooth fairy. Its name is Ratoncito Pérez, and it first appeared in the tales of Luis Coloma, a writer from the 19th century.

## The Spanish National Anthem Has No words

The majority of national anthems are meant to be hummed along to at least seem as if you know the lyrics while being sung and half-forgotten. In contrast, you won't have to bother memorizing anything in Spain other than the music of their national song. It formerly included words, but not any longer. It was composed in 1761 and is known as "Marcha Real." It is also among the oldest national anthems in the world.

## Spain Has the Most Bars of Any EU Member State

With all its pubs, you'd assume Ireland would win that honor, but Spain has the most bars per capita in the EU. Here, you may participate in some enjoyable pub crawls.

**Spain's Coastline Extends Over 8,000 Kilometers.**

Going to the shore is one of the most romantic things to do in Spain. And there are many beaches with all that coastline. One of our favorite things to know about Spain is that it boasts more than 8,000 beaches. That equates to around one beach every kilometer.

**The Spanish tradition of siesta is still very much alive.**

Knowing about the siesta may lead you to believe that it is kind of a stereotype, but it is not. We're going to explain what a siesta is if you're wondering what it is. An afternoon siesta is a snooze. maximum of twenty minutes. The whole nation is impacted since many businesses shut for siesta time between 2 and 5 p.m...
There is still work to be done on Barcelona's Sagrada Familia.

The renowned cathedral in the city, which Antoni Gaud designed, has been under construction for more than 130 years.

It is anticipated to be finished in 2026. With 2.8 million visits a year, it is perhaps the most popular construction site in the world. The largest fresh food market in Europe is in Valencia.
The 8,000-meter-squared Mercado Central, which was created in 1914, is a fascinating example of Valencian Art Nouveau architecture. There are 900 booths inside offering everything from olives, wine, and spices to cold cuts, seafood, and cheese. It's a fantastic location in Valencia to visit.

**Spain Gets More Tourists Than The Number Of People Who Live There**

Spain has a booming tourism industry. The fact that tourism in Spain is so significant is not well acknowledged, however. The nation got 82.5 million visitors in 2018, making it the second-most visited country on Earth. 46.7 million people are living in Spain, thus visitors make up almost half of the country's population.

**Not All of Spain Is "Spanish"**

This is probably a mind-blowing truth about Spain, yet what you would have assumed to be a straightforward definition of Spain isn't that. It is composed of several autonomous communities, each of which is governed to a different extent.
Celts inhabit Galicia. Basque is a language unique to the Basque Country and all of Europe. Occitan and Catalan are spoken in Valencia, Catalonia, and the Balearic Islands. Amazingly fascinating.

**5-Day Itinerary For You!**

**Day 1**: Entry into Madrid Start your experience by immersing yourself in the dynamic city's history and culture when you get to Madrid, Spain's capital. Visit the majestic Plaza Mayor, which dates back to the 17th century, first thing in the morning. Discover the Madrid de los Austrias neighborhood's winding lanes and take in the Royal Palace's magnificent architecture.

Make your way to the famed Prado Museum in the afternoon. It is one of the best art museums in the world and is home to works by well-known painters including Velázquez, Goya, and El Greco. Take a leisurely walk in the lovely Retiro Park to unwind and take in the tranquil ambiance as you say goodbye to the day.

**Day 2**: Getting to Know Barcelona Take an early train to Barcelona, which is renowned for its distinctive mix of modernist architecture, active street life, and breathtaking beaches. Visit the magnificent Sagrada Familia, Antoni Gaud's masterwork and a defining image of Barcelona, to begin your day. Explore the Gothic Quarter's winding lanes, which are lined with quaint cafés, specialty stores, and stunning medieval structures.

Take a leisurely afternoon walk down the well-known La Rambla street, where you can take in the vibrant ambiance and savor delectable regional food at the Boqueria Market. Visit Park Güell to round off your day. This other masterpiece of Gaud's has fantastic vistas of the city as well as wacky architectural features.

**Day 3:** Flamenco and Moorish Heritage in Seville Fly to Seville, Andalusia's capital, to witness the dynamic energy of traditional flamenco and learn more about the city's extensive Moorish legacy. Visit the majestic Seville church, the biggest Gothic church in the world, first thing in the morning, then go to the top of the Giralda Tower for sweeping views of the city.

Explore Santa Cruz's picturesque neighborhood in the afternoon. It has quaint cobblestone lanes, lovely patios, and secret squares. Discover Seville's magnificent Alcázar, a royal residence famed for its Mudejar architecture and verdant grounds. Treat yourself to a genuine flamenco performance in the evening to experience the fervor and intensity of this classic Spanish art form.

**Day 4:** The Alhambra and Albaicn in Granada
Visit the city of Granada, which is known for its magnificent Alhambra Palace and its medieval Albaicn quarter. It is located at the foot of the Sierra Nevada mountains. Visit the Alhambra first thing in the morning, one of the world's best examples of Moorish architecture and a UNESCO World Heritage site. Discover the Generalife, a summer palace with lovely water features, as well as its majestic castles, elaborate gardens, and other attractions.

Wander around the Albaicn neighborhood's winding lanes in the afternoon to experience the city's old Moorish design. Take in the charming ambiance of this historic area while admiring the stunning views of the Alhambra from the Mirador San Nicolás. Don't forget to enjoy some classic tapas as well as the complimentary tapa, presented in the manner of Granada, which is a local favorite.

**Day 5**: Valencia's Beaches and Modern Architecture Fly to Valencia, a coastal city noted for its cutting-edge construction, active neighborhood, and stunning sandy beaches. Visit Santiago Calatrava's futuristic complex known as the City of Arts and Sciences first thing in the morning. Discover the eye-catching structures, such as the Oceanografic, which is Europe's biggest aquarium, and the Hemisfèric, which houses an IMAX theater and a planetarium.

Afternoon excursion to Valencia's historic district to see the majestic Valencia Cathedral, said to contain the Holy Grail. Discover the fashionable stores, inviting cafés, and bright street art that lines the Barrio del Carmen's winding lanes. Finally, decompress at a stunning beach in Valencia, such as Malvarrosa or El Saler, where you may swim, rest, or engage in some water sports.

You'll get the chance to discover Spain's cultural gems, breathtaking architecture, and picturesque landscapes with the help of this varied 5-day itinerary. Have fun exploring this fascinating nation!

**Traveling in Spain**

Travelers may easily tour Spain's many regions and cities thanks to the country's broad and diversified transportation system. Here is a thorough guide to traveling in Spain, whether you want to go to well-known locations like Madrid, Barcelona, or the stunning island of Ibiza.

• Air Travel: Thanks to Spain's well-connected network of airports, flying is an effective way to cover large distances or get to well-liked tourist attractions swiftly. Major international airports including Madrid-Barajas Adolfo Suárez Airport, Barcelona-El Prat Airport, and Palma de Mallorca Airport provide service to the nation. Ibiza Airport serves as a gateway to the breathtaking Balearic island of Ibiza. Several domestic airlines provide quick connections between cities.

• Trains: The national train operator, Renfe, runs Spain's dependable and vast rail network. Madrid, Barcelona, Seville, and Valencia are just a few of the important cities connected by AVE (Alta Velocidad Espaola) high-speed trains. With frequent top speeds of 300 km/h (186 mph), these trains provide a convenient and pleasant means of transportation. Access to smaller towns and rural regions is made possible through Renfe's operation of commuter and regional trains.

• Buses: Popular in Spain, buses provide comprehensive coverage throughout the whole nation, including both urban and rural regions. The largest bus operator, ALSA, has a vast network of lines that connects towns, cities, and even outlying villages. Bus travel is often inexpensive, and the buses are nice, with facilities like Wi-Fi and air conditioning. Buses may be slower than trains, particularly over longer distances, so keep that in mind.

• Metro & Public Transportation: The main Spanish cities, such as Madrid, Barcelona, and Valencia, all have effective metro systems that make getting about the city easy. With regular trains and interconnected lines, these metros are often the quickest and most effective method to get about the city. Furthermore, cities have well-established public transit networks, including buses and trams, that provide an affordable method to visit various areas and attractions.

• Rental cars: For those who value more freedom and independence, renting a vehicle might be a fantastic alternative. The well-maintained road system in Spain, which includes freeways and picturesque lanes, enables you to see the nation at your speed. However, bear in mind that owing to traffic and parking restrictions, driving in city centers might be difficult. It's often more practical to use public transit in large cities.

• Ferries and Boats: Ferries and boats are necessary if you want to go to any of the Spanish islands, like Ibiza, Mallorca, or the Canary Islands. Between mainland Spain and the islands, many ferry companies provide routes that allow for both passenger and vehicle transit. Particularly Ibiza has excellent boat connections that make traveling to and from the island simple.

• Local Transportation: Once you reach your location, you may use local transportation in any Spanish city or town. Depending on the locale, they could include buses, trams, or metro systems. In metropolitan regions, taxis, and ride-sharing services are also readily accessible, providing a practical means to cover short distances or go to particular locations.

The mix of transportation options that best meets your demands, your budget, and the distance you desire to go should be taken into account when organizing your schedule. Keep in mind to check prices, ticket availability, and itineraries well in advance, particularly during busy travel times. You may easily discover Spain's rich cultural legacy, breathtaking landscapes, and dynamic towns, including the alluring island of Ibiza, thanks to the country's well-connected transportation system.

**Chapter two**

**Planning Your Trip to Spain: A Comprehensive Guide**

A seamless and pleasurable vacation to Spain requires careful planning in many important areas. This all-inclusive book will assist you in efficiently planning your vacation to Spain, from selecting the ideal time to go and developing an itinerary to setting up lodging, transportation, and discovering the local way of life.

• Select the Ideal Travel Period: Spain has a Mediterranean climate with some regional differences. For seeing well-known tourist attractions, the spring (April to June) and autumn (September to October) seasons are great since they provide nice weather and fewer visitors. The summer months (July and August) are the busiest travel times due to the pleasant weather and crowded attractions. Spain's winter (December to February) is often moderate, making it a wonderful time to explore historical cities or go skiing in the Pyrenees.

• Select Your Destination: Spain offers a variety of locations, each with its appeal. Aside from the prospect of visiting beautiful islands like Ibiza, Mallorca, or the Canary Islands, think about the places you'd want to visit, such as Madrid, Barcelona, Seville, Valencia, or Granada. To help you plan your schedule, do some research on the landmarks, cultural sites, and activities that you are interested in each location.

• Make an Itinerary: Based on the locations you've decided to visit and the length of your vacation, make a thorough itinerary. Consider the distances between cities, keeping a balance between sightseeing and downtime. Give top priority to must-see sites and provide enough time for investigation. Allow yourself some leeway so you may welcome unplanned discoveries and ingratiate yourself with the community.

• Arrange Accommodations: To get the greatest deals, do your research and make reservations early. From affordable hostels and guesthouses to opulent hotels and resorts, Spain provides a broad selection of options. When choosing your lodgings, take into account the neighborhood, facilities, and accessibility to public transit. You may also look into unusual choices for a more immersive experience, such as reserving a room in a parador (an old government-run hotel) or a typical Spanish home.

• Traveling: Select the best means of transportation for your journey. Use Spain's effective rail system if you want to travel between cities, particularly across vast distances. High-speed connections between major cities are made possible by trains like the AVE that run quickly and comfortably. Buses are a cost-effective solution for traveling short distances or visiting remote regions. Renting a vehicle gives you the freedom and flexibility to explore off-the-beaten-path areas if you value independence and flexibility. Use public transit inside cities, such as metros and buses, or use taxis and ride-sharing services.

• Investigate Local Traditions, Etiquette, and food: Learn about regional traditions, etiquette, and food to better understand the diverse culture and customs of Spain. To improve your trip experience and converse with locals, learn a few fundamental Spanish words and phrases. To guarantee a courteous and pleasurable stay, familiarize yourself with the regional traditions, and eating schedules (lunch is normally about 2 pm, and supper is later in the evening).

• Examine Activities and Food: Spain is well known for its tasty and varied food. Look into and try local delicacies including paella, tapas, churros, and wines from the area. Participate in activities that showcase the culture of the area, such as seeing flamenco performances, going to your neighborhood market, or going to festivals and events.

• Pack Properly: Incorporate the weather prediction for your vacation dates into your packing list. Spain's towns and sights should be explored in comfortable walking shoes, light clothes, sunscreen, and a hat. If traveling in the winter or shoulder seasons, pack a light jacket and layers. Don't forget to pack any required travel papers, such as your passport, id, and travel insurance.

• Stay Informed: Check official government websites or get in touch with your neighborhood embassy or consulate to stay informed on travel warnings, entrance procedures, and security information for Spain. Before leaving, make sure you are aware of any COVID-19-related rules, including any testing and immunization requirements.

By carefully organizing your vacation to Spain, and taking into account these important factors, you'll be well-equipped to enjoy the lively culture, extensive history, breathtaking scenery, and kind people of Spain. Take pleasure in exploring the beautiful places Spain has to offer.

**Exploring Spanish Cities:**

Spain is a fascinating and varied nation, known for its deep cultural heritage, gorgeous architecture, and attractive landscapes. Spain has a variety of cities, from thriving metropolises to charming beach communities, all eager to be explored. We will examine some of the most alluring Spanish towns in our travel guide to Spain 2023, showcasing their distinctive landmarks, rich cultural traditions, delectable cuisine, and more. Set off on a tour of Spain's metropolitan wonders to experience the beauty and allure of this intriguing nation.

• Barcelona: Barcelona, which lies in Catalonia, is a city that skillfully combines history and contemporary. Admire Antoni Gaud's architectural marvels, including the spectacular Sagrada Familia and Park Güell. Visit the colorful La Rambla, which is dotted with street performers, boutiques, and cafés, and explore the historical Gothic Quarter with its winding medieval lanes. Don't pass up the opportunity to sample delectable Catalan food and take part in Barcelona's legendary nightlife.

• Madrid: Madrid, the capital of Spain, is a vibrant city with a plethora of cultural treasures. The Prado Museum, Thyssen-Bornemisza Museum, and Reina Sofia Museum all include top-notch art collections that contain works of art by notable painters. Visit the magnificent Royal Palace, stroll through the lovely Retiro Park, and savor traditional Spanish fare in the city's tapas bars, and eateries. You will be enthralled by Madrid's exuberant energy at every turn.

• Seville: With its extensive history and flamenco rhythms, Seville, the capital of Andalusia, has a certain appeal. Discover the majestic Alcázar of Seville, a palace that displays Moorish and Mudejar architecture. The

Seville church is a must-see; it's the biggest Gothic church in the world. Climb the Giralda Tower for stunning city views. Enjoy the traditional tapas and delectable Andalusian food while being submerged in the passionate flamenco mood.

- Valencia: Valencia, which is located on Spain's east coast, combines modernism with tradition. Discover the future City of Arts and Sciences, a masterwork of architecture that houses an opera theater, scientific museum, and planetarium. The majestic Valencia Cathedral and the Silk Exchange, both of which are UNESCO World Heritage monuments, may be seen as you stroll through the city's historic core. Don't forget to sample the delectable rice dish Valencian paella, which is recognized across the globe.

- Granada: This city at the base of the Sierra Nevada mountains is well known for its impressive Moorish past. The Alhambra, a magnificent palace complex with gorgeous gardens and elaborate architectural elements, is the gem in the crown of the city. Visit the magnificent Granada Cathedral while exploring the UNESCO-designated world heritage site of the Albaicn neighborhood's winding alleyways. Don't forget to take in the bustling ambiance and have some authentic tapas in the thriving Sacromonte neighborhood.

Bilbao is a city in the Basque Country that has recently experienced a spectacular makeover. For art lovers, a visit to the renowned Guggenheim Museum Bilbao, constructed by Frank Gehry, is essential. Explore the picturesque Old Town, also known as Casco Viejo, with its winding lanes and typical Basque pintxos bars while taking a walk along the Nervion River. Immerse yourself in the distinctive Basque customs and take part in the city's bustling cultural scene.

Spain's cities provide a staggering variety of experiences that fascinatingly combine history, art, culture, and food. The country's rich tapestry is enriched by the architectural marvels of

Barcelona, the cultural riches of Madrid, the passionate flamenco of Seville, the contemporary allure of Valencia, the Moorish legacy of Granada, and the creative revolution of Bilbao. Travelers are invited to immerse themselves in the lively culture and unparalleled beauty of this varied nation by reading our travel guide to Spain 2023, which offers a look into the charming places that are just waiting to be discovered. The towns of Spain will create a lasting effect on your trip, whether you are looking for architectural wonders, cultural immersion, gastronomic pleasures, or a combination of all of these.

**Top Madrid Attractions**

Spain's vivacious capital, Madrid, is home to a wealth of historical sites, top-notch museums, beautiful architecture, and a buzzing environment. We will examine some of the most popular Madrid attractions in our travel guide to

Spain 2023. Madrid provides a wide range of activities for visitors looking to immerse themselves in the rich legacy and energetic character of the city, from imposing palaces to renowned museums and gorgeous parks.

• Prado Museum: Visiting one of the best art museums in the world, the Prado Museum, while in Madrid is a must. The Prado Museum displays Spain's rich creative past by housing a large collection of European classics, including works by Velázquez, Goya, and El Greco. Admire classic works like Goya's "The Third of May 1808" and Velázquez's "Las Meninas," and take in the breadth of Spanish art history.

• Royal Palace of Madrid: The official home of the Spanish royal family, the Royal Palace of Madrid will transport you to a world of regal splendor. Enjoy the magnificent furniture, murals, and fine tapestries that decorate the sumptuous interiors. Wander through the immaculately maintained Sabatini Gardens and explore the Royal Armoury, which houses a sizable collection of weaponry and armor. The Royal Palace is a must-see sight due to its magnificence and historical importance.

• Puerta del Sol: Known as Madrid's central plaza, Puerta del Sol is a busy gathering place and a center of activity. Observe the famed New Year's Eve events as residents assemble to ring in the new year, marvel at the unique Tio Pepe sign, and stop by the historic Kilometer Zero plaque marking the center of Spain's radial road system. Explore the nearby streets, which are dotted with stores, cafés, and historical sites.

• Retiro Park: This beautiful park, a big green oasis in the middle of Madrid, is the perfect place to get away from the rush and bustle of the city. Take a stroll along the walkways shaded by trees, hire a rowboat on the tranquil Retiro Pond, and marvel at the magnificent Crystal Palace, a glass building housing exhibits of modern art. The park includes has famous Monument to Alfonso XII, statues, and wonderfully designed gardens. It's the ideal place to unwind and take in the scenery.

• Plaza Mayor: Enter the charming Plaza Mayor, a historic plaza that goes back to the 17th century, and travel back in time. Admire the magnificent architecture, highlighted by the beautiful Casa de la Panadera and its graceful arcades. At one of the outside cafés, have a meal or a cool beverage while taking in the lively ambiance. Throughout the year, Plaza Mayor serves as a location for several cultural gatherings and performances.

• Thyssen-Bornemisza Museum: The Thyssen-Bornemisza Museum, housed in the Villahermosa Palace, is a great place to continue your exploration of art. A substantial collection of European artwork from the Middle Ages to the 20th century is kept at this museum. Enjoy the works of art created by famous painters like Monet, Van Gogh, and Picasso. The museum is a must-visit for art fans because of its wide collection, which provides a thorough picture of art history.

The best places to see in Madrid capture the essence, history, and aesthetic heritage of the place. These sites provide an enthralling look into the cultural fabric of the city, from the famous Prado Museum to the royal Royal Palace, the busy Puerta del Sol to the tranquil Retiro Park, and the iconic Plaza Mayor to the magnificent Thyssen-Bornemisza Museum. Exploring these top destinations will certainly result in remarkable encounters and a greater understanding of Madrid's vibrant appeal in the travel guide to Spain 2023.

**Art & Cultural Scene in Madrid**

Madrid, the capital of Spain, is a vibrant center of art and culture that has enthralled tourists for centuries. Madrid provides a rich tapestry of cultural expression, from top-notch museums and art galleries to energetic theaters, music venues, and a dynamic street art scene. We will examine Madrid's art and cultural scene in our travel guide to Spain in 2023, emphasizing its best museums, historical sites, festivals, and more.

• Museo del Prado: The Museo del Prado, one of the most renowned museums in the world, is the gem in Madrid's artistic crown. There is a sizable collection of European artwork there, with a concentration on works by Spanish artists including Velázquez, Goya, and El Greco. Admire classic works of art like Bosch's "The Garden of Earthly Delights" and Velázquez's "Las Meninas." The extensive collection of the Prado offers a remarkable tour through art history that spans centuries.

• Reina Sofia Museum: The Reina Sofia Museum, which is devoted to modern and contemporary art, is a must-see for art lovers. It has an amazing collection, which includes "Guernica," the famous work of art by Pablo Picasso. Discover the creations of foreign painters like Francis Bacon and Mark Rothko as well as Spanish artists like Joan Miró and Salvador Dali. The museum is a recognized cultural icon in Madrid because of its varied exhibits and provocative installations.

• Teatro Real: The Teatro Real, Madrid's opulent opera theatre, offers a glimpse into the city's thriving performing arts sector. The Teatro Real presents operas, ballets, and classical music performances of the highest caliber and is renowned for its superb acoustics and spectacular productions. Attend a show by well-known performers to experience the intriguing ambiance of this historic theatre.

• Matadero Madrid: Matadero Madrid is a cultural hub that presents cutting-edge performance, design, and art. This interdisciplinary venue, housed in a former slaughterhouse, presents theatrical productions, concerts, festivals, and exhibits. Discover the bustling cultural programming that represents Madrid's cutting-edge inventiveness while taking in cutting-edge art installations and live music performances.

• Lavapiés Neighborhood Street Art: Lavapiés has become a thriving center for street art. Wander through its bright streets to see the eye-catching murals, graffiti, and urban art produced by both regional and international artists. For fans of street art, the neighborhood's multiracial vibe and creative energy make it an intriguing visit.

• Festivals and Events: Madrid is renowned for its vibrant festivals and events that honor tradition, art, and culture. Learn about the San Isidro Festival, which celebrates Madrid's patron saint with music, dancing, and traditional attire. A wide range of international films are shown during the Madrid International Film Festival. The Veranos de la Villa festival presents a varied schedule of outdoor concerts, theatrical productions, and dance events in different locations across the city over the summer.

The colorful tapestry of Madrid's art and cultural scene displays the city's rich history and innovative energy. The city provides a wide variety of creative experiences, from world-class museums like the Prado, Reina Sofia, and Thyssen-Bornemisza to modern cultural places like Matadero Madrid. Madrid is a cultural treasure trove that will excite and enthrall tourists in Spain in 2023, whether they are examining works of art by famous painters, taking in live events, or learning about the dynamic street art scene.

**Gastronomy and Nightlife in Madrid**

Madrid is not just a city of art and culture, but it is also a popular destination for foodies and partygoers with a variety of tastes and inclinations. Madrid has a thriving and diversified culinary and nightlife culture, with everything from traditional Spanish food to cutting-edge dining experiences, from little tapas cafes to energetic clubs and pubs. This travel guide to Spain 2023 will examine the city's delectable cuisine and vibrant nightlife, emphasizing its best eating establishments, regional specialties, hippest clubs, and more.

• Traditional Gastronomy: Traditional Spanish cuisine has a strong influence on Madrid's gastronomic scene, which has a delectable selection of delicacies. Enjoy the famous Cocido Madrileo, a substantial stew made with chickpeas, or try the delicious Cochinillo, a roast suckling pig. The traditional bocadillo de calamares, a sandwich stuffed with crunchy squid rings and a local favorite, is not to be missed. To experience the true tastes of Madrid's cuisine, visit old pubs and family-run eateries.

• Mercado de San Miguel: Visit this ancient market, noted for its lively food vendors, for a gourmet excursion. As you take in the bustling ambiance, sample a variety of tapas, fresh seafood, charcuterie, cheeses, and other specialties. The market provides a gastronomic trip via various flavors and textures, ranging from traditional Spanish delicacies to cosmopolitan cuisines.

• Michelin-Starred eating: Madrid is home to some recognized restaurants that push the frontiers of culinary innovation. The city also has a booming Michelin-starred eating scene. Experience the highest caliber of gourmet perfection by learning about the innovative meals created by famous chefs. Madrid's Michelin-starred restaurants provide memorable dining experiences for food connoisseurs, including molecular gastronomy and avant-garde presentations.

• Tapas Culture: Madrid is known for its delicious tapas, so visiting the city's tapas bars is a must. You may discover a ton of bustling pubs serving a variety of tapas as you go through areas like La Latina and Malasaa. Try classic dishes like jamón ibérico (Iberian ham), tortilla espaola (Spanish omelet), and patatas bravas (spicy fried potatoes). As you go from pub to bar, sampling the delicacies and mingling with people, take in the friendly ambiance.

• Rooftop pubs and Terraces: Go to Madrid's hip rooftop pubs and terraces to experience the city's thriving nightlife. Drink beverages and take in the vibrant environment while taking in the expansive views of the metropolitan skyline. Madrid provides a variety of alternatives to suit diverse interests, from exclusive rooftop lounges to stylish patio bars. After a day of touring, it's the ideal place to relax and take in the city's dynamic vitality.

• Flamenco performances: Enter the passionate world of this essential component of Spanish culture. Flamenco performances may be seen in a variety of places throughout Madrid, from little tablaos to large theaters. Witness the exciting environment that is produced by the fascinating dancing, passionate vocals, and complex guitar melodies. Watch a mesmerizing flamenco performance to experience the soul-stirring rhythms of this legendary art form.

- Exciting Nightclubs: Madrid is known for having a vibrant and diversified club scene. The city has a vast variety of nightclubs that appeal to various musical styles and preferences. Madrid has something for everyone, from major dance clubs to underground electronic music venues. Make lifelong memories in the vibrant nightlife of the city, dance the night away to the rhythms of famous DJs, or take in live performances by regional and worldwide performers.

The cuisine and nightlife of Madrid are a dynamic combination of tastes, sensations, and entertainment. Madrid welcomes tourists to revel in its gastronomic pleasures and enjoy its dynamic nightlife. From cozy tapas restaurants to chic rooftop lounges and exciting nightclubs, Madrid offers a variety of delectable culinary options. Madrid will satisfy and excite you in Spain 2023, whether you're a foodie or a partygoer.

## Barcelona: The Mediterranean Gem

Barcelona, Spain's vivacious capital of Catalonia, is a Mediterranean treasure that mesmerizes tourists with its distinctive fusion of tradition, modernity, and culture. This in-depth travel guide to Spain in 2023 will examine the city of Barcelona's architectural wonders, breathtaking beaches, must-see attractions, attractive waterfronts, and mouthwatering culinary pleasures.

• Barcelona is known for its stunning architecture, with the Sagrada Famlia serving as perhaps its most recognizable example. This basilica, created by the brilliant architect Antoni Gaud, is a marvel of modernist construction, with ornate facades, towering spires, and a captivating interior. Another of Gaud's creations, Park Güell, is a whimsical space with striking sculptures, vibrant mosaics, and panoramic views of the city. Casa Batlló and Casa Milà, two of Gaud's domestic masterpieces that highlight his avant-garde and organic design aesthetic, should not be missed.

• Beaches: Barcelona, which is located on the Mediterranean coast, is home to some beautiful beaches where tourists can unwind and enjoy the sunshine. The most well-liked beach is Barceloneta Beach, which is renowned for its energetic ambiance, beach bars (chiringuitos), and water activities. For families and anyone looking for a more relaxing experience, Nova Icaria Beach provides a more serene environment. Locals love Bogatell Beach because it has a lovely length of golden sand.

• Must-See attractions: Barcelona has a multitude of must-see attractions in addition to Gaud's architectural marvels. The Gothic Quarter, also known as Barri Gtic, is a maze of ancient alleyways, old buildings, and picturesque squares. The Picasso Museum is one of the largest collections of famous artists' works, showing the early creations that influenced his creative development. tourists may explore sights like Montjuc Castle and the Magic Fountain on Montjuc Hill, which provides tourists with panoramic views of the city.

• Waterfronts: Barcelona's waterfront neighborhoods are lively and welcoming, providing the ideal balance of entertainment and leisure. La Barceloneta promenade is a well-liked location for a leisurely walk or a bike ride along the beach since it is dotted with eateries, cafés, and stores. The city's former port, Port Vell, has been upgraded into a contemporary waterfront with a marina, a retail mall, and the renowned Maremagnum complex. To see Barcelona's skyline from the water, take a boat excursion.

• gastronomic Delights: Foodies will appreciate Barcelona's gastronomic scene. The city provides a vast selection of delectable foods, ranging from traditional Catalan fare to delicacies from across the world. Try the renowned tapas, which are little plates of delectable savory treats like patatas bravas, calçots, and gambas al ajillo. Experience delicious fresh seafood at the thriving Boqueria Market, which is off La Rambla. Visit the city's Michelin-starred restaurants for a taste of contemporary Catalan cuisine, where outstanding chefs combine tradition and innovation.

- La Rambla: La Rambla, one of Barcelona's most well-known streets, is a bustling avenue lined with flower stands, boutiques, cafés, and street performers. It extends from Plaça de Catalunya to the waterfront Christopher Columbus Monument. Take in the bustling atmosphere as you stroll down La Rambla, browse the market booths, and stop at places like the Wax Museum and the Liceu Opera House.

- Nightlife: Barcelona has a renowned nightlife that offers a diverse range of activities for night owls. The city is well-known for its thriving bar culture, with hip cocktail bars and inviting taverns in areas like El Raval and El Born. Discover the live music venues in the city to see performances of jazz, flamenco, or modern music. For an amazing evening, visit one of the many bars and discos in the vibrant neighborhood of Eixample or the seaside clubs of Port Olympic.

Barcelona is a city that provides a genuinely magical experience, with its architectural wonders, stunning beaches, must-see attractions, attractive waterfronts, and gastronomic pleasures. Barcelona offers visitors to Spain in 2023 an amazing trip, whether they want to explore Gaud's remarkable masterpieces, unwind on the Mediterranean coastlines, delve into the dynamic culture of the Gothic Quarter, or indulge in the city's culinary riches.

## Chapter Three

## Exploring the Gothic Quarter:

## Immerse Yourself in Barcelona's Historic Heart

The charming district that makes up Barcelona's historic core is the Gothic Quarter, or Barri Gtic in Catalan. The Gothic Quarter provides a distinctive and charming ambiance with its winding, small alleyways, ancient buildings, and rich history. We will explore the Gothic Quarter's attractions in detail in this thorough tour, showcasing its architectural masterpieces, hidden jewels, cultural icons, and lively atmosphere.

Stepping inside the Gothic Quarter is like entering a time capsule because of its history and architecture. The neighborhood's history dates back to the Roman Empire, and tourists are still enchanted by the medieval buildings. Discover the secret squares and Gothic-style structures that border the twisting, confined lanes. Take in the beautiful facades of the Church of Santa Maria del Pi and the Barcelona Cathedral (Catedral de Barcelona). Visit the serene Plaça Sant Felip Neri, which has a somber past and bears testimony to the Spanish Civil War.

• Plaça del Rei: Located in the Gothic Quarter, King's Square is a hidden treasure. The Chapel of Santa Gata and the Palau Reial Major (Royal Major Palace), two outstanding architectural masterpieces, are located in this lovely area. Discover the MUHBA (Museu d'Histria de Barcelona), an underground archaeological monument that provides insight into Barcelona's Roman history. Explore the well-preserved medieval buildings and interactive displays to find out more about the city's past.

• Barcelona Cathedral: A beautiful Gothic masterpiece, the Barcelona Cathedral is often referred to as the Cathedral of the Holy Cross and Saint Eulalia. The Gothic Quarter's skyline is dominated by its spires. Enter to take in the interior's grandeur, which is enhanced by beautiful stained glass windows and elaborate decorations. Visit the cloister, which has a serene courtyard and a lovely fountain populated by 13 geese, representing the era of Saint Eulalia.

• Plaça Reial: Located immediately off La Rambla, Plaça Reial (Royal Square) is a lively public space. It was created by Gaud's contemporary Francesc Daniel Molina and has beautiful architecture, palm palms, and elaborate lampposts. On one of the outside decks, have a meal while sipping a beverage and taking in the energetic ambiance. The renowned Sala Apolo, a well-liked location for performances and club nights, is also located on the plaza.

• Museums and Cultural Centers: Several museums and cultural institutions that provide insights into Barcelona's past and present may be found in the Gothic Quarter. Visit the Barcelona History Museum to learn more about the city's history via interactive exhibitions and archeological artifacts. Explore the wide collection of sculptures, works of art, and historical objects on display at the Museu Frederic Marès. Contemporary art and culture are the subjects of the exhibits, performances, and activities held at the Barcelona Center for Contemporary Culture (CCCB).

• Hidden Gems: The Gothic Quarter's secret locations and hidden nooks are part of what makes it so alluring. Discover the beautiful boutiques, small cafés, and architectural marvels on the little streets like Carrer del Bisbe and Carrer dels Boters. Find the lovely Plaça del Pi, where the Church of Santa Maria del Pi is the center of attention. Explore Carrer de Petritxol, a neighborhood known for its quaint chocolateries and art shops.

• Dining and Shopping: The Gothic Quarter is a haven for foodies and shoppers alike. One of Barcelona's biggest shopping avenues, Portal de l'ngel, offers a mix of well-known worldwide brands and regional stores. In the maze of alleyways that encircle Plaça Sant Josep Oriol, find handcrafted goods, jewelry, and clothing. The Gothic Quarter has a wide variety of eating alternatives, including both traditional Catalan cuisine and tastes from across the world. Discover the evocative tapas bars, inviting cafés, and fine dining establishments hidden in its streets.

In summary, Barcelona's Gothic Quarter encourages tourists to take a trip through time and get fully immersed in the city's magnificent architecture and rich history. When visiting Barcelona in Spain in 2023, visitors should not skip the Gothic Quarter because of its interesting neighborhood, which has secret squares, historic buildings, and cultural treasures. Discover its hidden treasures, get lost in its allure, and take in the lively atmosphere that makes it such a unique area of the city.

**Seville: Andalusia's Enchanting Capital - Discover its Historic Landmarks**

Spain's Andalusia region's capital city of Seville is a compelling travel destination renowned for its deep cultural heritage, breathtaking architecture, and fervent flamenco. This thorough guide to Seville provides an in-depth examination of this wonderful city by taking you on a tour through its historical sites, charming neighborhoods, artistic legacy, traditional food, and colorful festivals.

• Alcázar of Seville: The Alcázar is a magnificent royal palace that displays a fusion of architectural styles, including Moorish, Gothic, and Renaissance influences. It is one of Seville's most recognizable buildings. Discover its exquisite gardens, which are decorated with fountains, courtyards, and luscious vegetation. Admire the Palacio de Don Pedro's delicate detailing, the Patio de las Doncellas' outstanding Mudéjar architecture, and the exquisite tile work that can be seen all across the complex. A must-see destination, the Alcázar is a UNESCO World Heritage site.

- La Giralda and the Cathedral of Seville: The Cathedral of Seville, often referred to as the Cathedral of Saint Mary of the See, is the biggest Gothic cathedral in the whole world. Take in its magnificence, ornate stained glass windows, and Christopher Columbus's grave. For sweeping views of the city, climb the old minaret known as the La Giralda Tower. The cathedral's dominance over the metropolis is evidence of Seville's long history and skill as an architect.

- Barrio Santa Cruz: This attractive area of Seville is known for its winding alleyways, quaint plazas, and typical Andalusian architecture. Explore its maze-like alleyways, which are covered with vibrant bougainvillea and charming courtyards. Discover the stores, tapas restaurants, and traditional flamenco venues at Plaza de los Venerables, Plaza Santa Cruz, and Callejón del Agua. This old area perfectly encapsulates Seville's rich cultural legacy.

• Plaza de Espaa: Situated within Maria Luisa Park, Plaza de Espaa is a lovely plaza. Its round structure, which was constructed for the Ibero-American Exposition in 1929, has a central fountain, tiled alcoves that symbolize several Spanish regions, and elegant bridges. Rent a rowboat and explore the canal that surrounds the plaza after taking a leisurely walk around the area and admiring the ceramic tile work.

• Triana: The thriving neighborhood of Triana is located across the Guadalquivir River. Triana, well-known for its vibrant architecture, rich flamenco history, and dynamic environment, provides a window into Seville's traditional and creative side. Discover its pottery studios, shop for regional specialties at the Triana Market, and see genuine flamenco performances in one of its many tablaos. Don't overlook the breathtaking city views from the Triana Bridge.

• Metropol Parasol: Located in the center of Seville, the Metropol Parasol, also known as Las Setas de la Encarnación (Incarnation's Mushrooms), is a stunning example of contemporary architecture. This creative wooden building incorporates a market, an archaeological museum, and an elevated promenade with sweeping city views. Due to the Metropol Parasol's flawless melding with its historic surrounds, it has come to represent modern Seville as an iconic emblem.

• Semana Santa and Feria de Abril: Seville is renowned for its colorful festivals, with Semana Santa (Holy Week) and the Feria de Abril (April Fair) being two of the most important. A somber religious holiday known as Semana Santa, processions weave through the streets as traditional music and the scent of the incense is played. In contrast, a week-long celebration of flamenco costumes, music, dance, and Andalusian culture is known as the Feria de Abril. Enjoy the spirited ambiance of this spectacular festival, the horse parades, and the casetas (decorated tents).

Seville, with its historical sites, charming neighborhoods, artistic legacy, and energetic festivals, is a city that perfectly encapsulates Andalusia's diverse cultural history. Seville provides a completely immersive experience, from discovering the architectural marvels of the Alcázar and the Cathedral to getting lost in the lovely lanes of Barrio Santa Cruz and seeing the fervor of flamenco in Triana. Enjoy the traditional food, soak in the wonderful atmosphere, and bask in the friendliness and charm of this charming capital city.

## Chapter four:

## Spain's Natural Beauty

The different landscapes of Spain's natural beauties are a treasure trove, ranging from craggy mountain ranges to unspoiled coasts, lush valleys to enormous deserts. This thorough book will take you on a tour of Spain's natural beauties, emphasizing the country's national parks, gorgeous beaches, alluring islands, and distinctive ecosystems. Discover Spain's stunning natural surroundings to understand why it is a haven for nature lovers.

• Picos de Europa: The Picos de Europa National Park, a mountainous beauty in northern Spain, is home to some of the most striking natural settings in the nation. Outdoor enthusiasts are treated to a breathtaking background of towering peaks, narrow gorges, and verdant valleys. Explore the scenic Covadonga Lakes, embark on hiking routes that lead to panoramic overlooks, and be in awe of the Cares Gorge's limestone cliffs. A wide variety of plants and animals, including the critically endangered Cantabrian brown bear, may be found in the park.

• Teide National Park is a UNESCO World Heritage Site and is home to Spain's highest peak, Mount Teide. It is located in the center of the Canary Islands. The lunar-like topography, vibrant mineral reserves, and famous Teide volcano make the volcanic scenery breathtaking to see. Explore the park's hiking paths, which are abundant with rare flora and animals, and take a cable car to the peak for breathtaking views of the neighboring islands. With its bright sky and observatories, the park is a stargazer's heaven.

• Costa Brava: The Costa Brava, a breathtaking coastal area in northern Spain, is renowned for its craggy cliffs, secret bays, and turquoise seas. Discover charming villages like Tossa de Mar, which has a medieval stronghold overlooking the sea, or Cadaqués, which has whitewashed buildings and meandering lanes. Explore remote beaches like Cala Pola or Aiguablava and partake in water sports like kayaking or snorkeling. Beachgoers and outdoor enthusiasts are drawn to the Costa Brava by its stunning natural surroundings.

• Sierra Nevada: Located in southern Spain, the Sierra Nevada mountain range is a breathtaking natural playground. It draws hikers, climbers, and nature enthusiasts since it is home to Mulhacén, the highest mountain in mainland Spain, and because it is a national park. Discover the lovely white towns and terraced fields of the Alpujarras area. The Sierra Nevada transforms into a well-liked ski resort throughout the winter, providing a variety of slopes for skiers of all abilities. It is very mesmerizing to see the snow-capped peaks against the clear sky.

• Balearic Islands: Known for their immaculate beaches, crystal-clear oceans, and picture-perfect scenery are the Balearic Islands, which include Mallorca, Menorca, Ibiza, and Formentera. The Serra de Tramuntana mountain range and magnificent bays like Cala Mondragó may be found in Mallorca. Menorca is a UNESCO Biosphere Reserve and has undeveloped beaches including Cala Macarella and Cala Mitjana. Salt flats, pine woods, and undiscovered bays are all part of Ibiza's unique environment. With its Caribbean-like beaches and pristine seas, Formentera draws tourists.

• Doana National Park: Situated in southwest Spain, Doana National Park is a hotspot for biodiversity and one of the most significant wetlands in all of Europe. Investigate its lagoons, dunes, and marshes, which are home to many different bird species, including flamingos and herons. To see the endangered Iberian lynx or the magnificent Spanish imperial eagle, join a guided trip. The park has been designated a UNESCO World Heritage Site because of its distinctive environment and conservation efforts.

• Timanfaya National Park: Located on the Canary Island of Lanzarote, Timanfaya National Park has a bizarre volcanic terrain resembling a lunar landscape. Discover the park's surreal landscape of lava fields, volcanic cones, and geothermal displays. Discover the unusual plants and animals that have adapted to this harsh climate by taking a guided tour. At the park's restaurant, where food is prepared using geothermal heat, you may experience the might of the Earth.

In conclusion, Spain's various landscapes and abundant biodiversity are clearly shown by the country's natural beauty. Spain has a staggering variety of natural treasures, from the rough Picos de Europa mountains to the gorgeous Costa Brava beaches, the volcanic landscapes of the Canary Islands to the distinctive marshes of Doana National Park. Spain's breathtaking natural beauty will capture your senses and leave you with priceless memories, whether you're looking for adventure, leisure, or the opportunity to immerse yourself in breathtaking nature.

**Marbella: A Glamourous Costa del Sol City**

Marbella, which is situated on the bright Costa del Sol in southern Spain, is known for its elegance, glitz, and energetic way of life. This thorough guide will take you on a tour of Marbella's lavish attractions, from its luxury resorts and glitzy nightlife to its immaculate beaches and top-notch golf courses. Learn why folks looking for a taste of the good life choose Marbella as their favored location.

The Golden Mile: The Golden Mile in Marbella is a section of upscale property that connects Marbella and Puerto Banus. Luxurious villas, lavish hotels, and private resorts border this famous neighborhood. Enjoy the stunning views of the Mediterranean Sea while strolling along the promenade dotted with palm trees. The Golden Mile is a paradise for anyone looking for luxury since it also has Michelin-starred restaurants, high-end spas, and designer shops.

- Puerto Bans: The opulent marina in Marbella and one of the most well-known sailing locations in Europe is Puerto Bans. Discover the marina's opulent yachts, upscale clothing stores, and trendy waterfront eateries. Take a stroll down the promenade of the marina and take in the energetic ambiance. Puerto Bans is a hotspot for nightlife as well, with exclusive clubs and nightclubs that draw international jet-setters and celebrities.

• Beaches and Beach Clubs: Marbella is home to several immaculate beaches with beautiful seas and gorgeous dunes. Popular beaches like Playa de Nagüeles or Playa Fontanilla are great places to relax. Marbella has many expensive beach clubs for people looking for an opulent beach experience. Enjoy a day of luxury sunbathing, cocktail-sipping, and fine dining while taking in the stunning views of the Mediterranean Sea. Among the most well-known beach clubs in the region are Ocean Club Marbella and Nikki Beach.

• Golf Paradise: Marbella is a golfer's dream, with a large selection of top-notch courses set against breathtaking scenery. Golf lovers may indulge in their passion on one of the more than 70 golf courses in the area, including championship courses created by well-known architects. Real Club de Golf Las Brisas, Los Naranjos Golf Club, and La Quinta Golf & Country Club are a few famous venues. Golf enthusiasts and pros from all over the globe go to Marbella.

• Old Town (Casco Antiguo): Marbella offers a lovely and historic aspect in addition to its reputation for excellent amenities. Discover Casco Antiguo, the Old Town of Marbella, with its winding lanes, charming plazas, and typical Andalusian structures. Visit Plaza de los Naranjos, the center of the Old Town, to take in the lovely orange trees, old structures, and charming cafes and stores. Discover the Marbella Castle, which offers sweeping views of the city, and the Roman Villa Ruins.

• Fine Dining: Marbella offers a broad variety of delectable cuisines, making it a heaven for foodies. Numerous Michelin-starred restaurants can be found in the city, where top chefs produce culinary wonders. At famous restaurants like Dani Garca Restaurante, Skina, or Messina, indulge in delectable Mediterranean cuisine, fresh fish, and foreign tastes. The eating scene in Marbella blends style, originality, and the best ingredients to produce genuinely remarkable dishes.

• Marbella International Film Festival: Every year, Marbella plays home to this festival, which draws actors, directors, and movie buffs from all over the globe. The festival celebrates the art of cinema in a glam environment by showcasing a wide range of international features, documentaries, and shorts. Watch movies, attend red-carpet events, and take advantage of networking chances to experience the thrill of the big screen at this famous festival.

For those looking for a rich lifestyle and a taste of the better things in life, Marbella is a popular destination due to its grandeur and glitz. Marbella provides a refined and affluent experience with its famed Golden Mile, glitzy Puerto Banus harbor, immaculate beaches, top-notch golf courses, and exciting nightlife. Marbella on the Costa del Sol guarantees a spectacular and opulent vacation, whether you're indulging in gourmet cuisine, seeing the ancient Old Town, or mixing with the rich and famous at exclusive beach clubs

**Exploring the Charming White Villages**

Spain is recognized for its beautiful scenery, extensive history, and dynamic culture. A collection of charming white towns are dispersed around the nation within this tapestry. These charming communities, hidden among rolling hills, offer gorgeous white-washed homes, winding cobblestone alleys, and an alluring mix of traditional and contemporary Spanish life. We cordially welcome you to travel through the quaint white villages of Spain featured in our travel guide to Spain 2023, where it looks as if time has stopped and the very best of Spanish culture is alive and well.

• Ronda: A jewel placed spectacularly on the rim of a ravine, Ronda is a city in the province of Malaga. The El Tajo Canyon's famous Puente Nuevo bridge, which spans this city, provides stunning views of the surroundings. Explore the famous Arab Baths, admire the Plaza de Toros bullring, and uncover the Moorish influence in the old town's winding lanes. Ronda is the ideal fusion of unmatched natural beauty, extensive history, and classic Spanish charm.

• Mijas: This Costa del Sol community is tucked away and is known for its picture-perfect white cottages that are embellished with colorful flower pots. Visit the Church of the Immaculate Conception, stroll through the quaint alleys on foot or on a leisurely donkey ride, and sample the regional food. Mijas is the perfect place to relax and take in the Spanish sunlight because of its expansive views of the Mediterranean Sea.

- Frigiliana: Tucked away in the Axarquia region's hills, Frigiliana is a charming town distinguished by its maze-like alleyways lined with colorful flowers and ornate ceramic tiles. Explore the historic district at your leisure, stop at the old Moorish stronghold, and look at the local crafts. The annual Three Civilizations Festival in Frigiliana adds a special cultural dimension to your trip by celebrating the coexistence of Christian, Muslim, and Jewish civilizations.

- Vejer de la Frontera: A lovely hamlet with expansive views of the Atlantic Ocean, Vejer de la Frontera is perched on a hill in the province of Cadiz. Explore its winding lanes, gaze at the beautifully maintained medieval buildings, and stop by the Church of the Divine Savior. Considering that the hamlet is also well-known for its food, make sure to sample some of it, particularly the legendary Retinto beef.

- Setenil de las Bodegas: Located in the heart of Andalusia, Setenil de las Bodegas is a unique location known for its cottages carved out of the rocks. Explore the intriguing caverns that have been transformed into pubs and restaurants, meander around the little lanes that twist between the cliffs, and go to the Church of Nuestra Seora de la Encarnación. A remarkable combination of history, scenic beauty, and gastronomic pleasures can be found in Setenil de las Bodegas.

Finding Spain's lovely white villages is a trip rich in fascinating history, magnificent scenery, and the friendliness of Spanish culture. Each town has its unique charm and appeal, giving visitors an insight into the region's rich history. Spain's white villages are certain to make an unforgettable impression on your travels in 2023, whether you're drawn to the dramatic scenery of Ronda, the rustic charm of Mijas, the charming streets of Frigiliana, the panoramic views of Vejer de la Frontera, or the unusual rock dwellings of Setenil de las Bodegas. Create lifelong memories by immersing yourself in the timeless beauty and authenticity of these hidden jewels.

## The Canary Islands: A Piece of Atlantic Paradise

The Canary Islands are an idyllic group of islands in the Atlantic Ocean located off the northwest coast of Africa. This Spanish archipelago consists of seven major islands, each of which has its distinctive collection of natural treasures, varied topography, and a comfortable environment all year long. We encourage you to experience the fascinating beauty and limitless opportunities that the Canary Islands have to offer by using this thorough guide.

The biggest of the Canary Islands, Tenerife, is home to a variety of attractions. Spain's tallest peak and a gorgeous volcano, Mount Teide, is its crown gem. Experience stunning vistas of the island by taking a cable car journey to the peak. Discover the magnificent woods and secret beaches of the UNESCO Biosphere Reserve Anaga Rural Park. Discover the colorful Santa Cruz de Tenerife, the island's capital and home to the world-famous Carnival, and relax on the Playa de las Teresitas' beautiful sands.

• Gran Canaria: Visitors are drawn to Gran Canaria by the variety of its scenery, which ranges from glistening dunes to lush woods and craggy cliffs. Visit Maspalomas, which has spectacular dunes, and Las Palmas de Gran Canaria, two charming villages. Learn about the quaint community of Teror, which is renowned for its colonial architecture and spiritual history. Experience the beauty of nature at the Roque Nublo, a famous natural rock structure, and the Caldera de Bandama volcanic crater.

• Lanzarote: With its surreal vistas sculpted by volcanic activity, Lanzarote mesmerizes visitors.

The lunar-like environment of Timanfaya National Park, where geothermal displays emphasize the island's volcanic activity, may be seen there. Discover the extraordinary Jameos del Agua, a natural cave that has been turned by famous artist Cesar Manrique into a place for culture and the arts. Enjoy the excellent food of the island while relaxing on Playa Blanca's gorgeous beaches.

• Fuerteventura: Home to extensive expanses of golden sand and beautiful seas, Fuerteventura is a beachgoer's and watersports enthusiast's dream come true. Discover the unspoiled shorelines of Corralejo, Costa Calma, and Sotavento, where kites and windsurfers delight in the optimum circumstances. Visit the charming town of Betancuria, featuring traditional Canarian architecture, and explore the stunning dunes of Corralejo Natural Park.

La Palma sometimes referred to as the "Beautiful Island," is a paradise for lovers of the outdoors. Discover the Caldera de Taburiente

National Park's UNESCO Biosphere Reserve, a volcanic crater with stunning scenery and hiking routes. Due to the island's minimal light pollution, go stargazing at the astronomical observatory Roque de los Muchachos. Discover Santa Cruz de La Palma, a charming village distinguished by its vibrant façade and cobblestone alleys.

- La Gomera: With its lush woods, deep ravines, and lovely communities, La Gomera provides a peaceful haven. Discover the mysterious Garajonay National Park's old laurel forest, a UNESCO World Heritage Site. Learn about Silbo Gomero, a rare whistling language that UNESCO has designated as an Intangible Cultural Heritage. Hike around Valle Gran Rey's magnificent scenery to discover the island's relaxed attitude.

- El Hierro: The smallest and most isolated island, El Hierro, provides a beautiful natural setting. Dive into the abundant marine life-filled, crystal-clear waters that surround La Restinga

Marine Reserve. Discover the wild terrains of Roque de la Bonanza and Timijiraque, as well as the exceptional juniper woodlands of El Sabinar. Visit the quaint hamlet of La Frontera and savor regional specialties like the famed queso de El Hierro cheese.

Stunning landscapes, rich cultures, and year-round good weather come together in the Canary Islands, which are a paradise in the Atlantic. This archipelago provides a wide variety of activities, whether you're looking for excitement, leisure, or a combination of the two. The Canary Islands attract visitors with their natural beauty and friendly hospitality, from the majestic Mount Teide on Tenerife to the lunar vistas of Lanzarote, the golden beaches of Fuerteventura, and the lush woods of La Palma. Travel to this magical location to learn about the countless joys that the Canary Islands have in store for you.

**Chapter five**

**Immersive Cultural Experiences: Unveiling the Soul of Spain**

Spain has a long history, many different customs, and a strong sense of cultural heritage. Beyond its well-known tourist destinations, Spain's genuine core is found in its rich cultural experiences. We welcome you to explore the rich fabric of Spanish culture by going beyond the obvious in this thorough travel guide. You may connect with Spain's heart and soul via these immersive experiences, which range from flamenco dance to delectable cuisine and centuries-old customs.

• Flamenco in Andalusia: Enter the passionate world of this historic art form, which has its roots in the region of Andalusia. Visit the thriving, flamenco-rich towns of Seville, Granada, and Jerez de la Frontera. Attend a live flamenco performance in a small tablao or visit Triana in Seville to see spontaneous performances in neighborhood taverns. Feel the beat, feel the passion, and let the eerie melodies and deft footwork take you to the heart of Andalusia.

• La Tomatina Festival in Buol: Take part in the thrilling mayhem of La Tomatina, a tomato battle that is celebrated all over the globe and takes place in the town of Buol, close to Valencia. Every year, on the last Wednesday in August, a huge tomato fight takes place in the streets with thousands of participants. Throw ripe tomatoes at other partygoers as you dive into the sea of red, letting go of inhibitions and embracing the happy atmosphere of this special celebration.

• Pamplona's Running of the Bulls: Take part in this renowned event, which takes place during the San Fermn festival and is filled with tradition and excitement. Join the courageous and daring as they run with the bulls through the streets in a breathtaking display of bravery and excitement. Wearing white clothing and a red neckerchief, immerse yourself in the festival's vibrant atmosphere and join in on the fun that happens after each day's bull run.

• La Rioja Wine Tasting: Travel through the famous wine area of La Rioja, where vineyards around the lovely scenery. Wine tastings in bodegas, or wineries, are facilitated by skilled sommeliers. Enjoy the distinctive aromas of Rioja wines, known for their depth and complexity, while learning about the winemaking process from grape cultivation to fermentation. Immerse yourself in the famed region's long history of winemaking and its cultural importance.

• Holy Week in Seville: Experience the breathtaking processions and passion of the religious celebrations of Seville's Holy Week, or Semana Santa. Witness the streets come to life as holy statues are carried on elaborately painted floats, accompanied by eerie music and the steady footfall of penitents. Follow the procession with the people, breathing in the aroma of incense and taking in the solemnity of this age-old custom. Discover the delicate craftsmanship of the floats and take in the enthusiasm of the community during this important cultural event.

• Culinary Delights in San Sebastián: Indulge in a gourmet adventure in San Sebastián, Spain's culinary capital. In the hopping pubs of the Parte Vieja (Old Town), sample pintxos, the Basque Country's take on tapas. Discover the bustling La Bretxa market, which is brimming with local specialties and fresh food. Take a cooking lesson to improve your expertise, discover the secrets of Basque cooking, and enjoy regional specialties like txuleta and bacalao al pil-pil.

• The Alhambra in Granada: Take in the breathtaking magnificence of this UNESCO World Heritage Site, which represents the height of Moorish design. Explore the elaborately tiled castles, gardens, and courtyards with their calming water features and gardens. Uncover the tales hidden inside this historical monument's walls to learn more about its importance and history. A fascinating look into Spain's heterogeneous history is provided by the Alhambra.

In conclusion, tourists have the chance to interact with Spain's rich legacy via its immersive cultural experiences, which reveal the nation's vivid character. These immersive events let you deeply interact with Spanish culture, whether you're drawn to the intense rhythms of flamenco, the excitement of La Tomatina, or the solemnity of Holy Week. If you fully immerse yourself in Spain's customs, celebrations, and cuisine, you'll come away with priceless memories and a profound understanding of the fascinating and varied cultural fabric of the nation.

## Understanding the Art of Bullfighting

Corrida de toros, sometimes known as bullfighting, is a contentious and long-standing institution in Spain. Bullfighting is regarded as an art form that blends athleticism, spectacle, and centuries-old traditions. It is rooted in both history and cultural values. We explore the history, components, and continuing controversy surrounding the art of bullfighting in this extensive note to give readers a better understanding of it.

• Origins and History: Bullfighting has its roots in several ancient ceremonies that included the sacrifice of bulls. However, it wasn't until the 18th century in Spain that bullfighting took on its current shape. It grew from conventional cattle-handling methods into an artistic performance that mesmerized spectators.

• Bullfighting's three main components, each having its own goal and spectacle, are as follows:

- Tercio de Varas (Lance Third): The matador and his crew evaluate the bull's strength and agility as it enters the ring. The bull is weakened by being lanced in the neck muscles by the mounted horsemen known as picadors, who also test the bull's courage and start the fight.

- Tercio de Banderillas (Banderillas Third): The matador pierces the bull's shoulders with colorful banderillas, and decorative poles with barb-tipped tips. The bull becomes even more vulnerable as a result, which causes it to charge harder.

- Tercio de Muerte (Death Third): In the decisive round, the matador faces off against the bull alone. The matador uses a cape to display his creativity, talent, and agility while making complex passes and movements. To display authority over the bull while avoiding harm is the goal. In the grand finale, the matador executes the estocada, a deadly sword thrust that is intended to kill quickly and precisely.

- The Matador's Role: The matador is the main character in a bullfight and is regarded as the epitome of courage, elegance, and talent. The art of the matador is to read the bull's behavior, react to it, and use calculated risk-taking and precise motions to provide an enthralling show. The crowd watches in awe as the matador displays his mastery of bullfighting tactics and control over the bull.

- Disagreements and Controversies: Bullfighting has long been a source of disagreement and discussion. Critics contend that it is an inhumane process that causes the animals involved needless pain. Bullfighting has come under fire from animal rights groups and campaigners, while some Spanish cultural and traditionalists have defended it. Both domestically and internationally, the discussion is still a sensitive one.

- Cultural Significance: Bullfighters claim that their sport is deeply established in Spanish heritage and is a unique type of art that honors the courage, tradition, and the special link between people and animals. They see bullfighting as a representation of Spanish culture and a long-standing custom that ought to be maintained.

The ability and talent required to understand the bullfighting art necessitate the recognition of its historical importance, as well as the current ethical discussions surrounding it. Bullfighting is still a complicated and debatable tradition, regardless of whether it is seen as an act of animal cruelty or a cultural display. The future of this ancient art form is unclear as Spain continues to debate the cultural and moral issues surrounding bullfighting.

# Wine and Cuisine

## Spain's Wine and Gastronomy: A Flavorful Journey

Spain is a place of superb wines and a treasure trove of gastronomic pleasures. Spain provides a rich and varied culinary experience, with everything from the sun-drenched Rioja vineyards to the hopping tapas restaurants of Barcelona. We cordially encourage you to explore the fascinating world of Spanish wine and cuisine in the extensive note that follows, learning about the famous wine regions, traditional foods, and distinctive cultural history that make Spain a genuine gastronomic paradise.

• Spanish Wine areas: There are several outstanding wine areas in Spain, each with its own unique terroir and grape varietals. Discover the beautiful red wine-producing Rioja vineyards, or go to the effervescent Cava-making Penedès area of Catalonia. Learn about the crisp whites of Rás Baixas and the robust reds of Ribera del Duero. Take in the tastes of Priorat, Montsant, and the other Andalusian areas. Each wine area has its allure and provides a chance to experience the true spirit of Spanish winemaking.

• Traditional Spanish food: The lively culinary traditions, robust tastes, and fresh ingredients of Spanish food are well-praised. Try traditional foods like paella, a delicious rice dish that is often enhanced with saffron and a variety of shellfish or meats. Enjoy the variety of Spanish tastes found in tapas, tiny plates that include traditional dishes like patatas bravas, jamón ibérico, and tortilla espaola. Don't pass up the chance to sample the hearty cocido madrileo, the rich stews of the Basque Country, and the fiery joys of Andalusian gazpacho. The voyage of flavor and joy that is Spanish food.

• Sherry and Andalusian Delights: In southern Spain, the region of Andalusia is well known for its famed fortified wine. Visit the Jerez de la Frontera vineyards, where the special Sherry manufacturing techniques have been refined over generations in the warm sun. Discover bodegas, get knowledgeable about the many Sherry types, and enjoy this distinctive wine's nutty smells and nuanced tastes. Sherry goes well with regional delicacies like tender jamón ibérico, delicately fried fish, and cool gazpacho.

• Cava and Catalan Cuisine: The sparkling wine known as Cava is found in Catalonia, the home of Gaud and thriving, international cities. Visit the Penedès area, which is just outside of Barcelona, and see how meticulously Cava is made. While you tour the vibrant food markets and enjoy Catalan cuisine, sip on these bubbly treats. Enjoy the tastes of fideuà (a seafood paella built with noodles), calcots with romesco sauce, and the well-known Catalan cream dessert.

• The Basque Country & Pintxos: The Basque Country is a must-visit location for food and wine enthusiasts because of its beautiful scenery and culinary skill. Discover the vibrant neighborhoods of San Sebastián and Bilbao, where the pintxos (Basque tapas) culinary tradition is alive and well. Enjoy the delicious delights offered at pintxos bars, which range from bite-sized treats like a grilled octopus to creative culinary fusions. Txakoli, a crisp and refreshing Basque wine, is the ideal accompaniment to these delicious snacks.

• Wine Festivals and Experiences: Arrange for your trip to take place during one of Spain's thriving wine festivals, such as the Haro Wine Battle in La Rioja or the Grape Harvest Festival in Jerez de la Frontera. Take part in wine tastings, vineyard visits, and other immersive activities that show you how wine is made. Engage with enthusiastic winemakers, discover the winemaking process, and learn more about the rich cultural legacy that Spanish wines are accompanied by.

The wine and culinary scenes in Spain are a genuine feast for the senses. Spain has a wide and enticing culinary environment, with everything from the world-class wines of Rioja and the elegance of Catalonia's Cava to the robust tastes of Andalusian Sherry and the creative pintxos of the Basque Country. Immerse yourself in the tastes, customs, and welcoming atmosphere of Spain, and set off on a wine and gastronomic adventure that will leave you with priceless memories and a deep respect for the nation's culinary legacy. Salud!

**Wine Regions and Tastings in Spain**

The unique terrain and extensive winemaking traditions of Spain are reflected in the region's world-famous wines, which are produced there. Spain is a wine lover's delight, offering everything from the lush green scenery of Galicia to the sun-drenched vineyards of Andalusia. We urge you to discover Spain's wine regions in this thorough overview, learning about their distinctive qualities, renowned wineries, and the memorable wine-tasting experiences that are waiting for you.

- Rioja: Rioja, in northern Spain, is one of the most well-known wine-producing areas in the nation. Rioja, which is renowned for its outstanding red wines, has a long history of wine production. Visit famous wines like Marqués de Riscal and Bodegas López de Heredia as well as the lovely towns of Haro, Logroo, and Laguardia. Attend wine tastings that focus on the classy Tempranillo grape and see how Rioja wines are traditionally aged in barrels to give them their characteristic flavor.

- Ribera del Duero: This region, which is nestled along the Duero River's banks, is well known for its production of strong, robust red wines. Discover the charming vineyards of the area where the Tempranillo grape, also known as Tinta del Pas locally, grows. Visit venerable vineyards like Vega Sicilia and Pingus and partake in tastings that highlight the area's superb workmanship. Learn about the distinctive tastes of Ribera del Duero wines and the love that goes into their making.

- Priorat: Priorat, a tiny but esteemed wine area in Catalonia, is home to some of Spain's most coveted and sought-after wines. The region's rocky landscape and soil, which is rich in slate, give its wines a distinct personality and minerality. Discover the old-vine Garnacha and Cariena vineyards that dot the steep slopes, and stop at famous wineries like Clos Mogador and lvaro Palacios. Participate in tastings to discover the depth and complexity of Priorat wines and appreciate the craftsmanship that goes into creating such exquisite expressions.

- Penedès and Cava: The Catalan region of Penedès is well-known for its still wines as well as for being the origin of Cava, a well-known sparkling wine in Spain. Visit the vineyards and subterranean wine vaults of Freixenet and Codornu, two Cava producers that scrupulously adhere to the traditional technique of production. Enjoy Cava tastings to experience the crisp, effervescent bubbles that have come to symbolize festivities in Spain.

- Sherry in Andalusia: Sherry, a fortified wine made in the region surrounding Jerez de la Frontera, is renowned across Andalusia. Explore this seaside region's traditional bodegas, such as González Byass and Bodegas Tradición. Experience tastings that highlight the many Sherry flavors, from dry and crisp Fino to lusciously sweet Pedro Ximénez, and learn about the distinctive Solera maturing technique. Discover the long history of Sherry manufacturing while savoring the classic aromas of this well-known Spanish wine.

- Wine Experiences and Festivals: In addition to the numerous wine regions, Spain conducts several wine events all year long. Consider timing your trip to coincide with occasions like La Cata del Barrio de la Estación in Haro, where street parties and wine tastings are common. Discover wine museums, vineyard tours, and educational seminars that provide an opportunity to meet dedicated winemakers and offer insights into Spain's winemaking traditions.

For wine lovers, Spain's wine regions provide a rich tapestry of tastes, customs, and immersive experiences. Each area has its distinct appeal, from the traditional elegance of Rioja and Ribera del Duero to the creative vitality of Priorat and the sparkling joys of Cava. Explore Spain's vineyards, indulge in wine tastings that highlight the variety of grapes grown there, and learn about the love that permeates each bottle. Spain's wine regions and tastings will leave you with priceless memories and a strong respect for the nation's vinicultural legacy, whether you are a beginner or an expert. Salud

**Tapas Culture and Gastronomic Pleasures**

The tapas tradition in Spain is a celebration of cohesion, friendship, and culinary creativity. Tapas bars, which serve a variety of delectable tiny dishes that tempt the taste buds, are an integral part of Spanish culture, from the crowded streets of Barcelona to the winding alleyways of Seville. In this extensive article, we dig into the dynamic world of tapas, examining its background, the range of foods available, and the distinctive cultural experience it offers visitors to Spain.

• The History and Tradition of Tapas: Tapas have a rich history and tradition. Tapas are said to have originated centuries ago when bartenders covered wine glasses with pieces of bread or ham to keep off dust and insects. These little nibbles were originally served with wine, but as the tradition developed, wine was added to encourage conversation and a feeling of community. Today, tapas have taken on a major role in Spanish cuisine, representing the spirit of camaraderie and sharing.

• Tapas come in a huge range of varieties that represent the regional tastes and ingredients of Spain. Each area has its unique cuisine, from the Andalusian gazpacho and tortilla espaola to the Basque pintxos and Galician pulpo a la gallega (octopus with paprika and olive oil). Enjoy fried calamari, patatas bravas, jamón ibérico, albondigas, and other delicious dishes. Whatever your taste, tapas provide a tempting assortment of options to please any palette, whether you love fish, meats, veggies, or cheese.

• Tapas Bar Culture: Any trip to Spain must include an immersion in the country's tapas bar culture. Explore the bustling atmosphere of tapas bars as you meander through the winding alleyways of medieval cities. Join the locals at the bar as they enjoy a variety of tapas while having vibrant discussions. Take a chance and sample the daily specials, which often include seasonal and local specialties. To enhance the taste and round out the experience, serve your tapas with a glass of regional wine, beer, or vermouth.

• Tapeo: The Art of Tapas Hopping: Tapeo, or the practice of visiting many tapas bars in a single evening, is a very Spanish experience. The streets of towns like Madrid, Barcelona, and

Granada are dotted with tapas restaurants, each of which serves a distinctive specialty. Go on a tapas trip where you visit several bars and sample different tapas at each one. Along with pleasing the taste, this culinary tour offers insights into regional culinary customs and friendly Spanish hospitality.

• Tapas with Michelin Stars: Although tapas bars are typically laid-back and informal, some chefs have raised tapas to the level of haute cuisine. Gourmet tapas that push the frontiers of taste and imagination are served at several Michelin-starred restaurants around Spain. At eateries like Tickets in Barcelona, Aponiente in Cadiz, and DiverXO in Madrid, sample the creative culinary fusions. These dining experiences provide a distinctive fusion of tradition and innovation, elevating tapas to a whole new standard of sophistication.

• Tapas Festivals: To properly experience tapas culture, plan your trip to coincide with one of the numerous tapas festivals held around Spain.

These gatherings honor the craft of creating tapas and provide a chance to sample a dizzying array of cuisine from across the world. Two thrilling events that highlight the inventiveness and flair of Spanish cooks are the National Tapas Competition in Valladolid and the International Tapas Competition in Lugo.

In summary, discovering Spain's tapas culture is a fascinating journey that appeals to all of your senses. The heart and spirit of Spanish cuisine are captured by this culinary heritage, from the long history and wide range of tastes to the friendly environment of tapas establishments. Enjoy a variety of small meals, enjoy the tastes of local delicacies, and embrace the idea of sharing and getting to know one another. You may fully experience Spanish cuisine by getting lost in the country's tapas tradition.¡Buen provecho!

## Traditional Spanish Dishes: A Culinary Journey through Spain's Gastronomic Heritage

Spanish food is recognized for its savory tastes, eye-catching hues, and a wide variety of regional delicacies. Spain provides a mouthwatering selection of traditional foods that represent its culinary past, from the fresh seafood of the coastal areas to the substantial stews of the interior. In this detailed note, we encourage you to take a gastronomic tour across Spain, discovering the recognizable and delectable traditional dishes that characterize the cuisine of the nation.

• Paella: Coming from the Valencian area, paella is perhaps one of Spain's most well-known foods. This saffron-infused rice meal is often prepared in a large, shallow pan with a variety of additions, such as chicken, rabbit, shellfish, or vegetables. The end product is a colorful and fragrant meal that perfectly encapsulates Spanish cooking. Enjoy regional varieties like black paella with squid ink or the traditional tastes of paella while taking in views of the Mediterranean shoreline.

• Gazpacho: This cool, revitalizing soup is ideal for Spain's hot summers. This colorful Andalusian meal is composed of bread, ripe tomatoes, cucumbers, bell peppers, garlic, olive oil, and vinegar. It is served cold after being blended to a silky consistency, giving off a blast of vibrant taste. Gazpacho is a refreshing dish to savor while you stroll through Seville's picturesque alleys or unwind in Malaga's sunny plazas.

• Tapas: Small appetizers or nibbles, tapas have come to represent Spanish cuisine. These bite-sized dishes have a variety of tastes and are great for sharing with friends. Enjoy a range of tapas, such as tortilla espaola (Spanish omelet with potatoes and onions), gambas al ajillo (garlic shrimp), pulpo a la gallega (Galician-style octopus), and patatas bravas (hot fried potatoes with aioli). Discover the exciting tapas culture in places like Granada, Barcelona, and Madrid, where tapas bars fill the streets and provide a delicious gastronomic experience.

• Jamón Ibérico: A sort of cured ham prepared from black Iberian pigs that are allowed to wander freely in Spain's oak woodlands, jamón ibérico is regarded as a delicacy. The distinct taste and softness of the flesh are a result of the pigs' diet of acorns. Enjoy the jamón ibérico's melt-in-your-mouth slices and appreciate its nutty, rich flavors. It is particularly excellent when paired with a glass of Spanish wine.

• Fabada Asturiana: This rich and soothing meal is from Asturias's northern area. Large white beans cured meats like chorizo and morcilla (blood sausage), and often pork shoulder or bacon are used to make this bean stew. It's a real treat because of the soft beans and slow-cooked spices. Try this renowned Asturian meal, which is a staple of the region's cuisine.

- Pisto: Popular across Spain, pisto is a tasty and adaptable vegetable stew. It is prepared by sautéing a mixture of bell peppers, tomatoes, zucchini, onions, and sometimes eggplant. Garlic, olive oil, and a dash of paprika are used to season it. Pisto may be eaten as a vegetarian meal or as a side dish to fish or meat that has been grilled. It is a cherished family favorite in Spanish homes due to its simplicity and rich ingredients.

- Churros with Chocolate: Churros con chocolate is a common Spanish delight that may be eaten for breakfast or as dessert to satisfy your sweet craving. When served with a thick and decadent hot chocolate dipping sauce, churros, which are fried dough pastries, are often dusted with sugar. Enjoy the delectable mixture by dipping the crisp churros into the silky chocolate. Take pleasure in this delectable dessert early in the day at a typical churrera or as a late-night treat after a night of flamenco dance.

In summary, traditional Spanish cuisine offers a gastronomic tour of the rich and varied tastes of the nation. Each meal in Spain tells a tale and represents the cultural legacy of its area, from the flavorful paellas of Valencia to the cool gazpacho of Andalusia and the delicious tapas found throughout the country. Immerse yourself in Spanish cuisine, tasting its genuine tastes and soaking up its welcoming atmosphere. ¡Good luck!

# Chapter six:

## Practical Information and Resources

A vacation to Spain demands thorough planning in addition to joy and expectation. We give helpful advice and useful resources in this extensive note to assist you in planning your trip to Spain in 2023. This book attempts to make your trip to Spain easy and pleasurable by covering all you need to know about important travel papers, modes of transportation, and helpful resources.

• Travel paperwork: Make sure you have all the required travel paperwork before departing for Spain. The majority of passengers will need a passport that is current and has at least six months left on its validity. You could additionally need a visa, depending on your nationality. To find out the precise criteria for your visit, contact the Spanish embassy or consulate in your country.

- Transportation: Spain has a well-developed transportation network that makes it simple to travel across the nation. Think about these choices for traveling around:

- Flights: Spain is home to several international airports, notably Barcelona-El Prat Airport and Madrid-Barajas Airport, which provide connections to important locations across the globe. There are additional domestic flights accessible for getting across Spain's many regions.

- Trains: Renfe, which runs Spain's huge and effective rail network. Major cities are connected by high-speed trains (AVE), enabling quick and pleasant travel. Regional trains run by Renfe are also great for visiting smaller cities, towns, and villages.

- Buses: In Spain, bus services are readily accessible and a cheap means of getting from one city or town to another. All around the nation, dependable and pleasant bus services are offered by organizations like ALSA and Avanza.

• Public Transportation & Metro: The metro systems in Spain's main cities, including Madrid, Barcelona, and Valencia, are well-developed, making it easy to get about cities. Local buses and trams are also effective forms of public transit.

• Car rental: Renting a car is a common option for traveling along picturesque roads and in rural locations. Major international automobile rental firms are active in Spain, which has a good road system. Make sure you are acquainted with the rules and regulations governing local traffic.

• Money and Payments: The Euro (€) is Spain's recognized unit of exchange. Airports, banks, and exchange offices all around the nation provide currency exchange services. Although most businesses take credit cards, it's always a good idea to have some cash on hand, particularly when visiting smaller businesses or rural locations.

• Language: Castilian Spanish is the official language of Spain. Even though English is widely spoken in tourist regions, learning a few fundamental Spanish phrases can improve your relationships with people and help you get through everyday problems more quickly.

• Safety and Emergency Services: Travelers usually believe Spain to be a safe destination. But it's always a good idea to exercise care. Watch out for pickpockets and keep a watch on your valuables, particularly in busy tourist locations. To get help in an emergency, use the 112 emergency hotline throughout Europe.

• Useful Resources: To improve your trip experience in Spain, make use of the following resources:

• Tourism Offices: Spain has a wide network of tourism offices that help visitors by giving them information, maps, and support. These places can assist you with itinerary planning and provide suggestions depending on your preferences.

• Online travel guides: Look through websites and online travel guides devoted to Spain. These websites provide in-depth details on locations, activities, lodging, and cultural experiences.

• smartphone applications: Use smartphone applications like Google Maps, TripAdvisor, and local transportation apps to identify attractions, navigate your way about, and get up-to-date information on bus and train timetables.

• Travel Insurance: Think about getting travel insurance to protect yourself from unforeseeable events like trip cancellations, medical problems, or misplaced luggage.

Conclusion: You may assure a smooth and pleasurable trip to Spain in 2023 by arming yourself with useful knowledge and using the tools at your disposal. Careful preparation can help ensure a great trip to this dynamic and varied nation, from setting up the required travel paperwork to investigating transit alternatives and accessing useful information. Get ready for a memorable journey packed with Spanish warmth, beautiful scenery, and rich culture. Happy travels! (Enjoy your journey!)

**Spain Accommodation Options: Choosing the Right Place to Stay**

Planning your vacation to Spain in 2023 must include selecting the appropriate lodging. There are several lodging alternatives available in Spain to accommodate every desire, spending limit, and vacation style. In this in-depth essay, we examine the numerous kinds of lodging that are offered, including anything from luxury hotels to affordable alternatives, attractive boutique hotels, vacation rentals, and more.

Learn about the finest possibilities for a relaxing and memorable visit to Spain.

• Hotels: Spain offers a diverse range of lodging alternatives, from opulent five-star hotels to more reasonably priced lodging. Large worldwide chain hotels with cutting-edge facilities and first-rate service are widely available in major cities like Madrid and Barcelona. Consider staying at a parador, which is sometimes housed in old structures like castles, monasteries, or palaces, if you're looking for a distinctive experience. Additionally, boutique hotels are well-liked options for tourists seeking quaint and chic lodging, especially in energetic areas.

• Vacation Rentals: For tourists looking for a more autonomous and at-home experience, renting a vacation house or apartment is a fantastic choice. A large variety of holiday rentals are available all around Spain on websites like Airbnb, HomeAway, and Booking.com. Vacation rentals provide the chance to experience local life while having more room and solitude, with options ranging from charming flats in the middle of cities to coastal villas and rural cottages.

• Hostels: Found all around Spain, hostels are great for tourists on a tight budget and those wanting a social environment. Hostels provide dormitory-style lodging with communal amenities such as kitchens, common spaces, and living rooms. For individuals who want more solitude while still taking advantage of the lively social setting, many hostels also offer private rooms. In places like Barcelona, Madrid, and Seville, hostels are especially well-liked and popular with backpackers and lone travelers.

• Rural Accommodations: If you're looking for a more sedate and genuine experience, think about staying in a rural lodging in a rural area or a tiny hamlet. There are several lodging alternatives available in rural Spain, including guesthouses, inns, and farm stays. While staying in attractive and bucolic locations, take in the stunning natural surroundings, immerse yourself in local customs, and sample regional food.

• Paradors: These distinctive lodging options are housed in old structures that have been turned into hotels. These businesses are often located in famous buildings like castles, monasteries, or palaces. When you stay in a parador, you may take advantage of contemporary conveniences and services while learning about Spain's rich history and architecture.

• Camping: Spain is a great place for campers because of its varied landscapes. There are many possibilities for camping in Spain, ranging from coastal campgrounds with views of lovely beaches to mountain campsites tucked away in the breathtaking Pyrenees. Showers, restrooms, and sometimes even swimming pools and recreational activities are available in campgrounds.

- Advice for Making a Reservation:

- Make reservations in advance, particularly during busy travel times and significant events.

- Examine evaluations and reviews to confirm the quality and dependability of lodging.

- Take into account the location and accessibility to facilities, public transit, and tourist sites that are significant to you.

To locate the greatest offers, compare costs and browse various booking services.

To meet the requirements and tastes of every tourist, Spain has a wide variety of lodging choices. There are several accommodations available to suit all travel preferences and price ranges, including luxurious hotels, affordable hostels, attractive vacation homes, rural lodgings, and distinctive paradors. Spend some time researching and choosing the ideal lodging that will improve your trip and guarantee a relaxing and enjoyable stay in Spain.

**Best Paradores in Spain:**

What exactly is a parador in Spain, you ask? And the solution is not too difficult. The Spanish government supports and sponsors special properties known as paradors, which may be translated straight as "hostels" in English.

To preserve, protect, and promoting Spanish travel, tourism, and hospitality, the Spanish government built a network of 97 state-run hotels. Visitors may stay at these hotels in a variety of accommodations. These extraordinary accommodations, which include castle hotels in Spain, palaces, monasteries, and castles, are often found in renovated historic structures. Convents and manor homes located on historical sites are also included.

The paradors, which are unlike any other Spanish hotel brand, are situated in picturesque, historically and culturally important locations. Spanish paradores, which originally appeared in 1910, have been open for business since their official opening in 1928.

Spain's paradors stand as a proud testament to its historical, cultural, and artistic legacy. By booking a stay at one of these excellent hotels, you can take advantage of first-rate lodging while also promoting genuine Spanish tourism.

Paradors of Alcalá de Henares, Cádiz, Cangas de Ons, Cardona, Chinchón, and Cruz de Tejeda, Cuenca's Paradoras well as other similar accommodations.

## Chapter Seven

## Using Language and Expressions

Travelers' Essential Spanish Phrases: Improving Your Experience in Spain

Learning a few fundamental Spanish words will significantly improve your travel experience when you set off on your trip to Spain in 2023. Even though English is widely spoken in tourist destinations, making an effort to converse in the local tongue shows respect and may foster closer relationships with locals. In this extensive note, we provide a compilation of crucial Spanish terms and phrases to help you get by in everyday encounters, order meals, get directions, and converse with people while visiting Spain.

• Greetings and Common Phrases:

- Hello: Hola

- Good morning: Buenos días

- Good afternoon/evening: Buenas tardes

- Good night: Buenas noches

- Please: Por favor

- Thank you: Gracias

- You're welcome: De nada

- Excuse me: Perdón/Disculpe

- I'm sorry: Lo siento

- Yes: Sí

- No: No

- Basic Conversation:

- What is your name?: ¿Cómo te llamas?

- My name is...: Me llamo...

- Where are you from?: ¿De dónde eres?

- I am from...: Soy de...

- How are you?: ¿Cómo estás?

- I'm fine, thank you: Estoy bien, gracias

- Nice to meet you: Mucho gusto

- Do you speak English?: ¿Hablas inglés?

- I don't understand: No entiendo

- Can you help me?: ¿Puedes ayudarme?

- I need help: Necesito ayuda

- I'm lost: Estoy perdido/a

• Can you repeat that, please?: ¿Puedes repetir, por favor?

• Ordering Food and Drinks:

• A table for [number of people], please: Una mesa para [number of people], por favor

• I would like...: Me gustaría...

• What do you recommend?: ¿Qué recomiendas?

• The bill, please: La cuenta, por favor

• Cheers!: ¡Salud!

• Do you have a menu in English?: ¿Tienes un menú en inglés?

• Can I have the check, please?: ¿Me puedes traer la cuenta, por favor?

• Water: Agua

- Coffee: Café

- Beer: Cerveza

- Wine: Vino

- Bread: Pan

- Fish: Pescado

- Meat: Carne

- Vegetables: Verduras

- Asking for Directions:

- Where is...?: ¿Dónde está...?

- How do I get to...?: ¿Cómo llego a...?

- Is it far?: ¿Está lejos?

- Turn left/right: Gire a la izquierda/derecha

- Straight ahead: Todo recto

- Bus station: Estación de autobuses

- Train station: Estación de tren

- Airport: Aeropuerto

- City center: Centro de la ciudad

- Excuse me, can you help me find...?: Disculpa, ¿me puedes ayudar a encontrar...?

- Emergency Phrases:

- Help!: ¡Ayuda!

- I need a doctor: Necesito un médico

- Where is the nearest hospital?: ¿Dónde está el hospital más cercano?

- I lost my passport: He perdido mi pasaporte

- I need to call the police: Necesito llamar a la policía

- Fire: Fuego

Remember that learning a few simple Spanish phrases may help you communicate effectively with locals and make lasting impressions when you are visiting Spain. Don't be scared to become involved in the local culture and adopt the language. When guests attempt to speak in their original language, the Spanish are noted for their friendliness and admiration.

Conclusion: By learning these fundamental Spanish expressions, you'll be better prepared for your trip to Spain in 2023. You'll be able to communicate with locals, ask for help, and navigate daily interactions. Respect the culture, embrace the language, and savor the rich experience of being immersed in the thriving Spanish-speaking world. Best wishes! Best of luck!

## Advice for a Smooth Trip

Making the Most of Your Travel Experience with These Spain Travel Tips

A trip to Spain is a thrilling adventure that offers a wealth of cultural experiences, breathtaking scenery, and delectable cuisine. It's crucial to plan and make the necessary preparations to guarantee a straightforward and enjoyable journey. In this thorough note, we offer helpful pointers and suggestions to make the most of your time in Spain while navigating your travels there.

• Planning and research:

• Research Spain's regions and cities to decide which locations you want to visit. Think about the historical, cultural, and natural sites that interest you.

- Check the weather and pack appropriately. Be ready for a range of temperatures and weather patterns because Spain's climate varies from region to region.

- Plan a thorough itinerary, but leave room for impromptu discoveries and unplanned detours.

- To respect the local culture and fit in, learn about the customs, traditions, and etiquette there.

- Safety and Travel Documents:

- Ensure your passport is valid for at least six months beyond your scheduled departure date.

- Determine whether you need a visa to enter Spain, and if so, apply well in advance.

- Make copies of your travel insurance policy, passport, and other crucial papers. Keep both physical and electronic copies.

• Register your trip with your embassy or consulate for any travel warnings or changes.

• Take essential care to secure your goods and personal safety. Be careful in busy situations and utilize lockers or safes offered by hotels for precious stuff.

• Transportation:

• Book your flights and lodgings well in advance for the greatest pricing and availability.

• Consider obtaining a transit pass or card, such as the Barcelona Card or Madrid Tourist Travel Pass, which gives savings and unlimited travel on public transportation.

• Familiarize yourself with the local transportation system, including trains, buses, metros, and trams. Use smartphone applications and maps to travel effectively.

• If going to drive, check you have an international driver's license and are acquainted with local driving rules and regulations.

• Communication and Language:

• While English is spoken in many tourist places, learning a few basic Spanish words may tremendously improve your travel experience and interactions with locals.

• Download a translation app or carry a pocket-sized phrasebook for easy reference.

• Consider obtaining a local SIM card or activating an international roaming plan for smooth communication throughout your vacation.

• Money Issues

• Become familiar with the Euro, the local currency, and exchange rates. For smaller businesses that may not take cards, carry some cash.

• To prevent any problems with card transactions, let your bank know about your trip intentions.

• Withdraw money from ATMs, which provide fair exchange rates. Pay attention to any transaction fees that your bank may charge.

• Dining and local cuisine:

• Enjoy Spain's cuisine by sampling regional delicacies and homegrown fare.

• Experience the tapas culture and savor tasty little meals with friends.

• Keep in mind that Spanish mealtimes are different from those in other countries. Dinner is normally provided starting at 8:30 p.m., while lunch is typically served from noon to 3 p.m.

- Respect regional traditions and manners:

- Recognize and respect regional traditions and customs. Learn about the proper conduct in religious settings and historic monuments, as well as cultural standards and clothing regulations.

- Be careful of noon closures in smaller towns and quieter areas as part of proper "siesta" etiquette.

- Pay attention to and abide by local laws and ordinances, such as recycling requirements and smoking bans.

- Health and Travel Insurance:

- Invest in full-coverage travel insurance to protect yourself from unforeseeable events like medical crises, trip cancellations, and misplaced bags.

- Always have a first aid kit and your necessary prescriptions with you.

- Become familiar with the addresses and phone numbers of the nearest medical institutions.

**Conclusion**: By using these helpful suggestions for a hassle-free vacation to Spain, you'll be well-equipped to travel across the nation, appreciate its unique culture, and make priceless memories. Be prepared, observe local traditions, and be open to new experiences. You may expect Spain's beauty, charm, and extensive history. Happy travels! (Enjoy your journey!)

Printed in Great Britain
by Amazon